Successful Library Fundraising

Successful Library Fundraising

Best Practices

Edited by M. Sandra Wood

ROWMAN & LITTLEFIELD
Lanham • Boulder • New York • London

Published by Rowman & Littlefield
A wholly owned subsidiary of The Rowman & Littlefield Publishing Group, Inc.
4501 Forbes Boulevard, Suite 200, Lanham, Maryland 20706
www.rowman.com

16 Carlisle Street, London W1D 3BT, United Kingdom

British Library Cataloguing in Publication Information Available

Library of Congress Cataloging-in-Publication Data

Successful library fundraising : best practices / edited by M. Sandra Wood.
    pages cm
  Includes bibliographical references and index.
  ISBN 978-1-4422-3738-4 (cloth : alk. paper) — ISBN 978-1-4422-3169-6 (pbk. : alk. paper) — ISBN 978-1-4422-3170-2 (electronic) 1. Library fund raising—United States. 2. Library fund raising—Case studies. I. Wood, M. Sandra.
  Z683.2.U6S83 2014
  025.11—dc23   2014011548

∞™ The paper used in this publication meets the minimum requirements of American National Standard for Information Sciences—Permanence of Paper for Printed Library Materials, ANSI/NISO Z39.48-1992.

Printed in the United States of America

Contents

Preface

Raising funds to support a library—whether it's an academic, public, or special library—is an ongoing issue; it's at the heart of the viability and future success of all libraries. And while libraries strive to provide the services, programs, and facilities that their patrons and communities want and need, funding is needed before these services, programs, and facilities can be offered.

Libraries obtain funding for operations in many ways—for example, through an institutional budget for academic libraries, or as part of a city budget for some public libraries. Some libraries organize annual campaigns for operations; some raise funds through book sales or special events. Funding is also needed for new buildings (capital campaigns), for special projects or services, and more. The list could go on and on. But, in most cases, libraries actively need to search for ways to fund their operation in the short and long term.

Successful Library Fundraising: Best Practices draws on the experience of librarians at twelve institutions to offer suggestions for raising funding and donations to cover operating expenses, special projects and services, handling capital campaigns, generating bequests and endowments, and working with library boards and foundations. All of these authors have successfully generated money and/or donations for their respective libraries utilizing both traditional approaches (e.g., book sales or author events) and newer electronic methods (e.g., websites, social media, and crowdfunding). Most have used a multi-pronged approach, looking at both immediate and long-term needs. All librarians should be able to take something from these successful efforts and apply them to their own libraries.

ORGANIZATION

Successful Library Fundraising: Best Practices consists of twelve chapters covering a wide range of funding activities by all types of libraries, both large and small, and all are written by experienced library fundraisers. The arrangement of the chapters reflects the variety, moving between public, academic, and special libraries, from traditional fundraising efforts to newer ones using online sourcing, from focused efforts to multifaceted ones.

In Chapter 1, Andy Kahan describes the Author Events Series at the Free Library of Philadelphia, provided through its foundation. This program, developed over many years, brings in nationally known authors and has been extended to larger events to fund library programs. Author Events celebrates its twentieth year in 2014; other events include a teen authors series and the Philadelphia Book Festival.

Tom Hadzor and Kurt Cumiskey describe the overall fundraising initiative at Duke University Libraries. Their program is multifaceted, including major gift prospecting, an annual fund, planned giving, and more. Their fundraising activities involve both traditional methods and newer technologies such as social media and utilizing the library's website, all of which are described in Chapter 2.

Jane Rutledge details the well-developed book sale program that provides major funding for the Tippecanoe County Public Library in West Lafayette, Indiana. Her account of how to run a book sale program provides wonderful tips for libraries that also use book sales to generate operating funds. She offers best practices and suggestions that include how to handle donations, pricing, organizing the sale, publicity, and working with volunteers and book dealers.

In Chapter 4, Dwain Teague tackles the difficult task of making discovery calls—that is, "cold calling" prospective donors to help generate both current and future funding for the library. He provides sample e-mails and "snail mails" that will help break the ice for these cold calls. In addition, he offers best practices to help librarians get started with building their donor bases, including meeting with prospects visiting the institution, meeting outside the library, and working with library staff.

Chapters 5 and 6 describe the Campaign for Seattle's Public Libraries, a major fundraising effort by the Seattle Public Library Foundation to raise capital funding for the SPL's main library and its branches, and for special programming and an endowment. In Chapter 5, Terry Collings describes the early years of the foundation and its structure, along with the initial campaign; as he shows, the campaign was years in the making. While not all libraries will have access to the major corporate donors, as was the case for the SPL, the campaign methods and practices described here are transferable for smaller-scale campaigns. Jonna Ward continues the SPL story in Chapter 6, describing how the Seattle Public Library Foundation then took its fundraising campaign to the community, seeking smaller donations from individuals and library patrons, thus involving everyone in this community effort. She provides a simplified work plan to help others with activities such as telefunding and direct mail.

Librarians at the Health Science Center Library at the University of Florida have used grants—both large and small—to provide programming and help fund staff. In Chapter 7, Hannah Norton and colleagues describe how initial success in finding grant support led to additional grant opportunities from within the institution and from outside sources, and outreach to other departments also opened up new funding. They offer a set of lessons learned to help others who seek to fund programs and services through grants.

In Chapter 8, Christina Muracco of the Smithsonian Libraries describes working with a library's board of directors. She covers the various roles of the board (and, specifically, its involvement in fundraising). Throughout the chapter she provides best practices for both board members and librarians working with board members.

Karlene Jennings tackles what some librarians may view as a difficult task—planned giving. In Chapter 9, she describes the need for tact and respect in working with potential libraries, looking at the long-range goal fundraising activity of generating bequests for the library. She covers basics and best practices for dealing with planned giving donors.

In Chapter 10, Sidney Berger describes fundraising efforts in special collections. He points out that fundraising is not always a money-raising effort—in some cases (and especially for special collections), it may be about outreach to generate donations of collections. He offers best practices for outreach to book dealers, collectors, authors, and more. This chapter highlights a case history of the exhibition of books from the University of California, Riverside (which houses the J. Lloyd Eaton Collection of Science Fiction, Fantasy, Horror, and Utopia), at the West Coast book fair of the Antiquarian Booksellers Association of America, which generated many donations to the library.

Gina Millsap and LeAnn Meyer show in Chapter 11 how important it is for a library to have a multifaceted approach to fundraising. They report how the Topeka and Shawnee County Public Library, in cooperation with Friends of the Topeka and Shawnee County Public Library and the Library Foundation, worked together to create a fundraising program that funded a new bookmobile, sought corporate sponsorship for a Literacy Partnership, began a program for planned giving, created an annual campaign, and more.

In the final chapter, Lee Price describes multiple uses of digital philan-thropy by libraries and library organizations—using the Internet for fund-raising through websites and tools such as social media and crowdfunding; as he says, "It's a new age." After describing several instances in which the Internet was used for fundraising, he offers ten tips for using the Internet to generate funds.

From traditional to new fundraising methods, from small to large libraries, from academic to public to special libraries—*Successful Library Fundraising* offers tips, suggestions, and best practices that you can adapt to use success-fully for your library.

Fundraising for Public Libraries with Author Events

ANDY KAHAN

Free Library of Philadelphia Foundation

A VERY GOOD PLACE TO START

Called "the region's preeminent forum for writers and ideas" by the *Philadelphia Inquirer*, the Free Library of Philadelphia's renowned Author Events Series brings internationally celebrated voices in the humanities and sciences to Parkway Central Library for great conversations with thoughtful readers throughout the Philadelphia region. Over the course of its twenty-year history, the Author Events Series has grown from a small, sporadic smattering of lectures to a much-loved, nationally renowned program. And with an online archive of podcasts from past events, the Author Events Series is reaching millions of people, building new and enthusiastic audiences around the world.

How has Author Events grown into the successful series that it is today? To answer that, we find ourselves first in fin de siècle Philadelphia, circa 1992. Bill Clinton has won the presidential election, and the administration of the Free Library of Philadelphia is in the midst of a five-year, long-range strategic plan to carry the institution and its burgeoning community of users into the twenty-first century by renovating each of the more than fifty neighborhood libraries through the *Changing Lives* campaign. As part of the campaign, the Free Library has designated outreach and public programming as a critical area that is to receive renewed attention and emphasis.

As we all know, outreach and public programming has long been a mainstay of public libraries—it's what we do. Remember the bookmobile? Remember when you attended your first story hour at your local library? The colorful illustrations, warm voice of the librarian, and friendly atmosphere allowed your imagination to wander during your journeys to outer space, your walks through the city with a certain mischievous monkey, or your sad recognition of loss as a tree gave every bit of herself to a demanding little boy who would become a man someday.

Library programs build on the connections established during the formative childhood years and prove indispensable as we age and grow. Simply stated, we continue to need the stories and the knowledge contained between the covers of books—whether the pages are virtual or actual. If story hours in libraries lead to a love of reading, and a love of reading leads to an interest in writers, then the most obvious place to find writers telling stories should be the library. Or so administrators who envisioned the Free Library's Author Events Series imagined. As we'll see below, they had good reason, given the institution's experience with presenting hundreds of thousands of programs since it opened in the early 1890s. Built in 1927, the Free Library's main location, the Parkway Central Library, has served especially as an incubator and presenter of innovative, literacy-based programming and outreach, burgeoning in the latter half of the last century.

In the late 1950s, the Free Library and the City of Philadelphia sponsored the Family Book Fair, a three-week extravaganza focused on books, reading, and, as the name suggests, the family. The fair featured film screenings, puppet shows, music performances, book signings, receptions, and author readings. Well-known writers, including Newbery Award winner Marguerite De Angeli (*The Door in the Wall*), Ingri and Edgar D'Aulaire (*D'Aulaire's Book of Greek Myths*), Edward Eager (*Half Magic*), and H. A. and Margaret Rey (*Curious George*)—there's that mischievous monkey, again—were but a few of the luminaries attending the fair, which was programmed in venues across the city.

Continuing to the 1960s and early 1970s, the Free Library offered a Current Scene lecture series, providing residents with insight into the cultural and political events of the time. "Life Stories: Biographies Brought to Life," a six-part series held in 1989, featured one-person shows focusing on important people in history such as Amelia Earhart, Eleanor Roosevelt, and Wolfgang Amadeus Mozart.

In the early 1990s, the Free Library cosponsored a highly successful event celebrating the publication of *Race-ing Justice, En-gendering Power*, a book of essays addressing issues raised by the Anita Hill and Clarence Thomas incident that occupied the national conscience for many years. The event featured a panel of eleven of the contributing essayists, including the book's editor, novelist Toni Morrison, who moderated the discussion.

With such strong programming as a launch point and a panoply of pending initiatives including the new strategic plan, renovation of the branches, and a focus on outreach, administrators felt the time was right to mount a new Author Events Series that would make the Free Library a beacon of culture in the city.

What's the Big Idea?

Looking for input from the community and to build consensus for the series, the Free Library formed focus groups to discuss the need for a major programming initiative and to consider the features the programming should include. The focus groups stressed the importance of bringing people to the library to "fire up their imaginations and fantasies" and "remind the community that the Free Library is a place of magic, of joy, of interest, of fun, and an institution that is more gloriously global than any other institution in town." The focus groups saw exciting, powerful public programming as an effective way to re-create and enhance that perception of the library among adults and to highlight the library as a central intellectual magnet for the community.

Following these public opinions, library administrators conceived the Library A-Loud program (subsequently renamed Rebuilding the Future and, finally, Author Events). The objectives of the program were to stimulate intellectual inquiry and understanding, debate, and the free exchange of ideas; to position the Free Library of Philadelphia as a vibrant center of intellectual activity and dialogue in the region; and to provide the public, which traditionally uses the library for quiet study, research, and pleasure, with the opportunity to engage actively with ideas and issues.

The Devil Is In

In order to launch the Author Events Series, the president and director of the Free Library of Philadelphia at the time, Elliot L. Shelkrot, worked with Kathy Gosliner, the Free Library of Philadelphia Foundation's director of development, to conceive, synthesize, and submit a grant to the redoubtable, Philadelphia-based William Penn Foundation. The grant contained the following concrete program initiatives (among others):

- Presentations, panel discussions, and debates by world-class authors, historians, political or media figures, creative artists, and other luminaries
- Interaction and debate among presenters and audiences
- Active engagement of the Free Library's branches to foster broad community participation
- Controversial issues and diverse groups coming together on neutral ground
- "Clusters" of events related to a primary topic to deepen understanding and enjoyment and to broaden participation
- Information, materials, and formats that connect program participants with Free Library collections

• A variety of formats, collaboration with other groups, scheduling that builds the expectation of regularity, and a component that allows spontaneous response to noteworthy events of the day

The Author Events Series would feature programs to be presented in four parts in the months of October, January, March, and May each year. Each presentation was to be supported by the aforementioned "clusters" of related events at both the Parkway Central Library and the branches throughout the city. These "clusters" were to include discussion groups, films, videos, readings, behind-the-scenes library tours, displays, and other activities.

Administrators outlined additional program objectives for succeeding years. During years two and three, the four-part series would be augmented by supplementary programs to be held during months when featured programs were not scheduled. These additional programs could include a response to a breaking event or a program with special relevance to the year's theme. The additional five programs would bring the total number of programs in the Author Events Series to nine.

Expected attendance at each of the four main events was projected at 300 people, or 1,200 people annually, with each cluster of branch events related to the main event expected to attract 500 people, or 2,000 annually, for a grand total of 3,200 people in the first year. In the second and third years, an additional 2,500 were projected to attend the five supplementary events each season for a grand total of 5,700 in attendance in the final year of the grant.

Also of note in the original conception of the Author Events Series, and of particular interest to those of you who have turned to this chapter, administrators felt that the new programs would give the Free Library the opportunity to test new ways to attract supporting revenues, including admission fees, VIP receptions, theme dinners, and special sales of books or other materials such as mugs, tote bags, and CDs.

Projecting a total budget in excess of $600,000 over three years to cover staff salaries, speaker fees, and series promotion and receptions, the Free Library requested and received more than $500,000 to launch the new series. The textbox shows a sample of the average annual budget of the Author Events Series in its early years, with the numbers rounded for ease of use. Administrators expected any difference in funding—if required—would be composed of corporate and individual gifts as well as single-ticket and series-package revenue.

When the Author Events Series began, the single-ticket price for the main events was set at $6.00—comparable to the cost (at the time!) of attending a movie—allowing a low barrier of access to the events for Philadelphians from across the economic spectrum. For attendees who wished to participate

---

AVERAGE ANNUAL BUDGET OF AUTHOR EVENTS SERIES

EXPENSE

- Salaries (two full-time employees): $70,000
- Presentations (Parkway Central and branches): $100,000
- Promotion (brochure, advertising): $15,000
- Support (ticket handling, freelance, telephone, supplies): $12,000
- Receptions (4 x $1,500): $6,000
- Total: $203,000

REVENUE

- Ticket Sales: $40,000
- Books and Merchandise: $8,000
- Corporate Sponsors and Individual Gifts: $30,000
- Foundation Grant: $125,000
- Total: $203,000

---

in a reception and support the Free Library with a greater fiscal commitment, the library created a series of subscriber package options to add value to the program and revenue for the institution. The packages included

- Season Package: $24.00 for four lectures
- Patron Package: $100.00 for four lectures and receptions
- Angel Package: $200.00 for four lectures and receptions, preferred seating, and recognition in the program booklets

Later seasons featured a Benefactor Package that doubled the benefits and costs of the Angel Package and included tickets to all of the speakers for the full year. Also in later years, a tax-deductible contribution to benefit Author Events was added to the cost of the packages to help sustain the program. The basic package and ticketing structure have remained largely unchanged, though fees (single tickets now cost $15.00), package names, and some benefits have shifted.

Reeling in the Years

While the first year of programming proved a rocky climb—it took more time to secure speakers and launch a program of the scope of the Author Events Series than initially anticipated—public response was positive. Attendance exceeded expectations at all of the main events by nearly 30 percent, filling (or nearly filling) the four-hundred-seat hall for each presentation. With an inaugural-year roster including E. L. Doctorow, Thomas Keneally (appearing only four days after *Schindler's List* received the Academy Award for Best Picture), and Susan Sontag, it's no wonder.

Year two began on firmer footing. A strong list of speakers, including Ken Burns, Sherwin Nuland, Wendy Wasserstein, and Gloria Naylor—along with the full implementation of cluster events around the main speakers (films, author primers, exhibitions, and panel debates) and programming throughout the fifty-four-branch Free Library system that amplified the themes of the speakers at the Parkway Central Library—pointed toward a more successful season.

In order to understand how clusters and themes were structured within the program framework, consider the events built around Gloria Naylor, bestselling author of *The Women of Brewster Place*. A few days prior to Ms. Naylor's presentation titled "Family Relations in Life and Literature," the library offered a free afternoon screening of Oprah Winfrey's film of the novel. Two days later, a local professor led a discussion group on the themes found in Ms. Naylor's various books. In the neighborhood branches, programming explored the novel's themes with topics such as "Family Life," "African American Tales," and "Family and Community." With the exception of Ms. Naylor's lecture, all of the events were free and open to the public. Attendance figures were

- Gloria Naylor, lecture: 370 (evening)
- *Women of Brewster Place*, screening: 70 (evening)
- Works of Gloria Naylor, discussion: 8 (daytime)
- Branch programs: 20 per event (various times)

As expected, attendance varied according to the time of day and event type, while the general pattern of attendance was similar for all of the main, cluster, and branch events around each author invited to speak that year.

Overall, the second season proved successful: attendance again exceeded expectations at all of the main events, with cluster and branch programs continuing to meet the audience participation established in the grant. While revenue from the corporate community was not as forthcoming as initially anticipated, ticket and package sales exceeded expectations and covered the revenue differential. Perhaps the most salient difference between the freshman and sophomore seasons was the addition of five more speakers to the Parkway Central roster, an eventuality planned for in the initial budgeting, but one that, in the end, did not require much additional spending.

"How is that possible?" you might ask. It turns out that the quality of the paid authors, number of attendees, good press, and strong on-site book sales achieved during the inaugural year of Author Events allowed administrators to make a solid case to the publishing houses in New York City to send a limited number of touring authors to the new series—thereby reducing program costs while increasing revenue.

At the time the Author Event Series began, Borders Books and Music and Barnes & Noble were hosting the "brand-name" authors when they passed through Philadelphia, so it was a bit of a coup for the Free Library to be considered a viable commercial venue. In fact, the leap to hosting touring authors, combined with the city's fortunate geographical placement between the standard book-tour stops of New York (where author tours are traditionally launched) and Washington, DC (a de facto stop for most well-known authors of fiction and, in particular, nonfiction), helped ensure the long-term success of the series.

Of course, it takes more than a good location to make a viable author program. It also helps to be in one of the top media markets in the country, which in turn allows the series advertising and publicity in print and on radio, television, and the web to reach and drive the potential audience to the events. (Conversely, no publicity = no audience = no book sales = no events!)

By the end of the third year of the series and the grant, a few facts had become clear: With eight of the nine speaker events sold out and the number of programs in the branches doubling in three years, the Author Events Series had become the vibrant center of intellectual activity and dialogue in the region that both the organizers and public had hoped. The local press paid attention to the series with coverage of events, and the series was playing a key role in the success of the Free Library's *Changing Lives* campaign, helping to raise both the visibility and the position of the institution as a worthwhile philanthropic choice.

TIP: INVOLVE A BOOKSELLER

Of equal or greater importance, a qualified bookseller is essential to have at events. The Free Library has been fortunate to have a long-term partnership with the Joseph Fox Bookshop, one of the oldest independent bookstores in the city—and one of the few left standing. Known for its knowledgeable clerks and hand-picked stock of quality fiction, nonfiction, art, design, and architecture books, the Joseph Fox Bookshop has been a reliable partner for the better part of two decades, ordering and selling books at each of the library's many events. The bookshop also reports its weekly sales (including books sold at author events) to four important bestseller lists: the *New York Times*, the *Wall Street Journal*, Indiebound, and Bookscan. When publishers know that sales at events count toward weekly bestseller lists, they are more likely to send authors to the venue. In short, consider working with your local independent bookstore—especially if they report to any of the aforementioned lists. Independent stores are also where you'll find the most knowledgeable and accountable bookselling staff.

Sowing the Seeds

The Author Events Series gave (and continues to give) the Free Library an opportunity to hold major donor cultivation events. Potential donors who might never visit the library for personal use were now attending dinners and receptions honoring famous speakers. Board members invited potential donors to attend events as a way to introduce them to the library and to encourage their support. Furthermore, the unique opportunity to meet and introduce onstage the authors who were appearing in the series had become an additional important entry point for new backing for the Free Library.

To wit, one avid supporter of the Author Events Series donated enough money to provide listening devices in the auditorium so that the hearing-impaired could take advantage of the series and other library events. By the end of the third year of programming, Author Events attendees had given more than $350,000 to the *Changing Lives* campaign, and five individuals who attended events had become members of the Free Library Foundation Board of Directors or the Free Library Board of Trustees.

The program also afforded the opportunity to cultivate major corporate and foundation gifts. Representatives of corporate and foundation philanthropies attended events and learned about the goals of the campaign. Several corporate gifts in excess of $100,000 for technology and renovations throughout the library system and one major foundation grant of $250,000 could be traced to the Author Events Series.

Events were also designed to thank important contributors. The Free Library held dinners for several of the authors to honor the institution's new George S. Pepper Society, named for the uncle whose $225,000 bequest enabled his nephew, Dr. William Pepper, to help found in 1891 "a general library which shall be free to all." Over time, the Pepper Society and the Author Events Series became mutually beneficial—Author Events offered Pepper members early access to tickets, priority seating, and receptions with authors, while the Pepper Society helped provide funding for the Author Events Series.

This nascent link between the society and the series was evident to administrators at the time the first grant for Author Events was expiring. What to do? *Carpe diem*, as Horace once wrote. And seize the day they did, returning to the William Penn Foundation for another three-year grant to keep Author Events viable. Fortunately, the foundation renewed their support, guaranteeing three more years of programming. However, it had become apparent that for Author Events to become fiscally independent in the future, the Free Library needed to build a separate endowment fund to maintain and perpetuate the series.

Administrators thought that the best way to begin building the endowment would be to offer prospective donors the opportunity to honor a living or deceased loved one with a special lecture as part of the Author Events Series. The gift would enable the donor to have an annual, named lecture as well as a dinner or reception at the Parkway Central Library with the author delivering the lecture. In addition, the honoree's name would appear on the event program, in advertisements, on the web, and in any additional collateral associated with the evening.

In 1998, during the fifth season of the program, the initial endowment gift of $125,000 was secured from a generous donor looking for a way to honor the memory of her mother. Other endowment gifts soon followed. In a little less than a year, another $400,000 (four endowments) had been pledged in support of the series. A final goal of $1.2 million was set with the thought that a combination of endowment, ticket, and package income would ultimately sustain the Author Events Series.

With $525,000 "in the door" and the endowment in need of another $700,000, administrators decided to speed the plow and applied to the National Endowment for the Arts (NEA) for a matching grant that would allow them to achieve the endowment goal by the time the second grant ended. Once the library received the NEA matching grant, its Development Department began actively soliciting new endowment donors. Although a number of Author Events supporters signed up to endow the series, the final goal of $1.2 million was not reached prior to the expiration of the second William Penn Foundation grant in 1999.

However, the gap between the goal and the current endowment didn't prove problematic. Due to a bit of canny planning by Richard Lippin, the first director of the Author Events Series, who retired in 2000, he was able to leave his successor with a $100,000 operating surplus composed of single-ticket and package revenue to continue the program into the next millennium.

The endowment for the series was eventually completed in 2003, with new endowments trickling in over the succeeding years as the program became more widely recognized and donors continued to wish to honor their loved ones.

MORE IS MORE

Cool Books, Hot Topics

A changing of the guard also led to a change in the form of the Author Events Series. At the time I took over as the new director, the series was limited to ticketed events and did not run into the summer. With a never-ending stream of writers on tour, why not begin a free summer program as a way to keep the public engaged with events throughout the year? Doing so would also fulfill one of the pillars of the initial grant: "scheduling that builds the expectation of regularity." The machinery of the program was already in place. The only things needed would be additional limited funding to pay for brochures, advertising, and author-related expenses of travel, hotel, and a small honorarium when the enticement was necessary.

With these thoughts in mind, the Free Library secured a three-year grant from the Independence Foundation and launched the Cool Books, Hot Topics free speaker series in the summer of 2001, under the Author Events Series banner. With tongue firmly in cheek, the Cool Books brochure offered residents air-conditioning along with the opportunity to engage in a dialogue with a favorite author or personality. The first season of Cool Books offered a plethora of highlights: eleven-time NBA Champion Bill Russell gave a great talk to fans (after ducking under every doorway that led to the stage); Zadie Smith offered an animated reading from her hilarious and affectionate masterpiece of polyglot London, *White Teeth*; Wynton Marsalis blew some cool jazz in between stories about his career, life on the road, and his eminent musical family; Provençal provocateur Peter Mayle eloquently schooled the audience in *French Lessons: Adventures with a Knife, Fork and Corkscrew* on some of the finer things in life; E. Lynn Harris talked to more than six hundred people who had lined up around the block to hear about his astonishing journey from self-published author (selling books from the trunk of his car) to bestselling phenomenon; and Jennifer Weiner, a reporter for the *Philadelphia Inquirer* who was about to become a nationwide bestseller with the book that launched her career, *Good in Bed*—now in its fifty-seventh printing—had the crowd in hysterics.

Free Events

The success of Cool Books, Hot Topics begged the question: Why not have free author events all year long? Additional authors could be added to the seasonal roster as revenue and calendar space permitted. Soon the Free Library was hosting free events year round in tandem with the ticketed events. Initially, administrators feared the free events would undercut ticket sales, but it became clear that there was an audience for both types of events—and in some cases, it was the same audience. The bottom line: Audiences were willing to pay to see the authors they loved (and authors they didn't love but wanted to tell their friends they saw first)—though they were just as happy to walk in the door without a ticket.

Free author events created goodwill in the community—thus staying true to the institution's name—while allowing diversity of programming in terms of topic and author stature. For example, audiences are willing to come out to support a well-known local author, but they aren't keen to pay; similarly, there are any number of terrific lesser-known writers to whom the Free Library can now offer access without the expectation of having to break even by selling an abundance of tickets and books. The library diversified the topics offered and featured presentations by local chefs and restaurateurs including Susanna Foo, Ellen Yin, Marc Vetri, and Jose Garces; musicians Daniel Bernard Roumain and the inimitable Little Jimmy Scott; birders Kenn Kaufman and Peter Dunne; and litterateurs Roberto Calasso and bell hooks, among many others.

With the new layer of free events, the series eventually ballooned from 12 or 16 authors a year to more than 120 per year—an intimidating number of programs for an office of two full-time and one part-time staff member.

Field Family Teen Author Series

In 2002, in response to the closure of libraries throughout the Philadelphia School District, the Free Library considered starting an author series especially for students, with the intent to bring classrooms of teens from local schools to their neighborhood library in order to foster familiarity with the branch as a nearby resource for study, homework, and recreational reading. Not long after the teen series was conceived, a couple at a reception for Garrison Keillor learned of the incipient series. Two years later, that couple provided pilot funding and then endowed the series in perpetuity, creating the Field Family Teen Author Series.

The endowment includes funding to cover hotel, travel, and honorariums for authors, personal copies of the featured books for each participating teen, and two staff positions: an outreach coordinator and an author coordinator. The outreach coordinator works with the administration at local schools and the branch heads of neighborhood libraries to bring classrooms of teens to the branches. The outreach coordinator also reads and recommends books for the Teen Author Series in consonance with the author coordinator and a small advisory team of administrators—including a teen specialist—who ultimately choose the titles and authors for inclusion. In order to avoid job duplication, the position of author coordinator has been subsumed into the position of associate director of author events. The position's duties include book selection, coordination of author travel, creation of collateral materials (brochure/author blurbs), and purchase of the author's books.

Today, the Field Family Teen Author Series operates in partnership with Philadelphia high schools and middle schools—public, charter, magnet, and diocesan—and is open to classes in grades 7–12. There is no cost to schools or students, and each student receives a free copy of the visiting author's book to keep. The outreach coordinator visits classrooms to talk about the author's book and delivers copies for each student to read in advance, and the best part—students meet the author at their local Free Library branch for a one-hour presentation, Q&A, and book signing. For most of these students, it is their first time meeting a published author; for some, sadly, the signed book they receive is the only book in their house.

In the decade since the Field Family Teen Author Series began, the library has brought tens of thousands of Philadelphia's young adults together with some of their favorite authors, including Walter Dean Myers, Lois Lowry, Markus Zusak, Laurie Halse Anderson, Orson Scott Card, Sherman Alexie, Ransom Riggs, R. J. Palacio, and John Green—to name more than a few. *School Library Journal* writes, "Philly's Free Library has created a teen program that would make Oprah envious" (McCaffrey, 2005).

Philadelphia Book Festival

Over the many years since the Free Library's first book festival, the Family Book Fair in 1959, a number of organizations in the city attempted to host book festivals with varying degrees of success. Unfortunately, most could not gain a toehold in the culture for more than a few years at a time.

Seeing an opportunity, the library created a free book festival in 2007 to be held over a weekend both outside and inside the Parkway Central Library during National Library Week. Outside, the festival would feature a vibrant street fair of literary vendors, self-published writers (renting tents and table space), stages for children's authors and musicians, a storybook character parade, a teddy bear picnic, a live simulcast of indoor events, and all manner of strolling entertainers, from jugglers to dancers to balloon sculptors. Inside the library, poets would declaim, artists illustrate, panelists point and counterpoint, and writers read. Book events would fill nearly every department and meeting space. The festival would be a celebration of literacy and the joy of reading, and a reminder of the library's importance to the community.

Vision in hand, the Development Department of the Free Library Foundation secured an initial grant from the John S. and James L. Knight Foundation. The Knight Foundation intended their gift "to highlight new possibilities that the Benjamin Franklin Parkway [the city's Champs-Élysées–like thoroughfare of arts and sciences] has to offer the region, both culturally and economically, by supporting the first annual Philadelphia Book Festival" (knightfoundation.org/grants/20070614/). With their motivation quantified, Free Library Foundation fundraisers next approached the corporate community, securing sponsorship from Target, Citi, Toyota, and GlaxoSmithkline, among other companies, along with the City of Philadelphia's blessing and support from the Philadelphia Industrial Development Corporation.

The Philadelphia Book Festival moved from the idea stage to the web as squibs about authors and musicians began to people our website. Sponsor branding soon followed, and designs, ads, flags, and stage banners materialized from screen to print. The leading sponsors (Knight, Target, Toyota, and Citi) had branded stages and tents lining the street in front of the library; Toyota brought along a selection of their latest automotive offerings, including the most recent version of the Prius; Target trucked in a trailer's-worth of little red chairs, various activities, and even a mini-bookstore.

The first Book Festival was announced with great fanfare: Three-time Caldecott Award winner David Wiesner designed the artwork that graced all of the posters and handouts (see Figure 1.1); KYW Radio and the 6ABC television station promoted the event through public service advertisements and agreed to report live from Parkway Central Library, interviewing key festival staff and talent; and the *Philadelphia Inquirer* and *Daily News* featured an eight-page color calendar pull-out with a listing of all events. With scores of

Figure 1.1.   David Wiesner Art/Poster Art. (Credit: Image courtesy of David Wiesner)

volunteers signed up to guide the public and a full roster of talent, there was nothing left to do but respond to the unpredictable and cross our fingers and toes with hope that the weather would hold.

It did.

More than 25,000 readers from Center City Philadelphia and adjacent counties traveled by foot, bus, trolley, car, and train to celebrate literacy during the two-day festival. Yes, there were many terrific writers: Alexander McCall Smith, Mary Higgins Clark, Terry McMillan, Ann Rule, Leslie Marmon Silko, Gary Shteyngart, Elizabeth Gilbert, Jerry Pinkney, and R. L. Stine; yes, there were gifted musicians: Patti Smith, Vieux Farke Toure, Jeffrey Gaines, Marta Gomez, literary band One Ring Zero (featuring Jonathan Lethem), and novelty band Harry and the Potters; but it was the commitment of the Free Library staff and of volunteer, corporate, and foundation support that made the festival possible.

And yet the description above does not do justice to the overwhelming organizational, logistical, and managerial oversight, the handshaking and wringing, and the endless e-mails, phone calls, and documents processed, signed, returned, and filed—not to mention all other manner of minutiae involved in creating a two-day indoor/outdoor literary event.

Of course, there were bumps along the way: authors and musicians were late; sometimes we had too many volunteers or too few; some people didn't check in when or where they were supposed to; and others were confused about which venue was which. But the event was still a great success.

How could we tell? We randomly surveyed our audience.

Of the nearly 400 people surveyed, 94 percent rated the festival "excellent" or "good." The Free Library gathered a wealth of additional data including zip code, topics of interest, gender, level of education, whether the respondent brought children, and how attendees learned about the festival. The most important number we needed to continue was the percentage in the first sentence above—that and renewed funding commitments from the various sponsors.

Encouraged by the Knight Foundation, which had sent a representative to attend the festival, our development officers immediately applied for a second grant. Within months the library received a letter notifying us that we had received a multiyear gift to sustain the festival for another three years. It appeared the days of the vanishing book festival in Philadelphia were over.

In the years since the first Philadelphia Book Festival in 2007, the economy endured one of the deepest recessions of the past one hundred years. While the festival continued strong with funding from Knight, fiscal support from both the corporate community and the city began to wane as the recession took hold of the bottom line. Of course, individual vendors who paid to participate felt a similar pinch.

In order to keep the festival alive, library administration gradually diminished the outdoor footprint of the festival, obviating the need to spend on city services (police, street closure, trash collection, electricity generation, and stage setup) as well as the cost of talent to equip, manage, and fill stages. Inside Parkway Central Library, fewer events were scheduled, although the headlining events in the auditorium continued apace.

With little fiscal support in sight, administrators leveraged the internal resources of the institution and, in a counterintuitive move, expanded the length and reach of the festival by having the neighborhood branches bring in local authors to give readings and talks while Parkway Central moved from a two-day to a seven-nights-in-a-row schedule of single, "tent pole" events with bestselling and/or prize-winning authors.

As with Cool Books, Hot Topics and the free author events throughout the year, the expenses for the Philadelphia Book Festival were eventually incorporated into the Author Events Series budget. Writers who appeared during the festival were included in Author Events publicity, outreach, and advertising schedules, and every participating festival author had to be on book tour at the time they appeared at the library in order to maintain affordability, as the library would not need to pay an honorarium for an already-touring author.

Despite the diminished size of the festival and limited number of authors, the gambit worked. By the time you read this, the library will have held its eighth annual Philadelphia Book Festival, featuring Pat and Gina Neely, Lydia Davis, Anne Perry, Debbie Macomber, and Barbara Ehrenreich, along with local authors throughout the neighborhood libraries, with a view toward festivals nine and ten. While attendance at the festival no longer reaches into the tens of thousands, the annual event still offers the library the opportunity to showcase the institution and welcome Philadelphians of diverse reading interests to celebrate literacy and a love of reading.

Author Events at Twenty

In 2014, the Author Events Series celebrated twenty years of literary excellence. Transitioning over time from a grant-funded experiment to a self-sustaining literary arts program with $200,000 in ticket sales and an annual budget of $400,000, the program has become the de facto venue in Philadelphia for great conversations with notable writers and thinkers.

The series audience has grown from 1,200 attendees at four main events when it began in 1994 to an annual audience in excess of 25,000. The local NPR station and major daily newspaper, the *Philadelphia Inquirer*, routinely review or interview authors appearing at Parkway Central Library, as do a host of other daily, weekly, and community papers, blogs, websites, cable and radio shows, culture sites, and online calendars. BookTV regularly broadcasts Author

Events lectures, helping to bring the series and the library to national attention; and the Author Events Series has gone global with more than 25,000 followers on Facebook and Twitter and 350,000+ Author Events podcasts annually downloaded around the world.

High-profile events over the years with Richard Clarke (audience of 500) a few days after he testified before the 9/11 Commission; Barack Obama (see Figure 1.2; audience of 700), who filled Parkway Central when he stopped by to discuss and sign his book *The Audacity of Hope*; and Ms. Bossypants herself, Tina Fey (audience of 900: 600 at the library, 300 across the street at a live simulcast), who grew up in a nearby suburb—along with recent off-site events for Pete Townshend (audience of 800), Sheryl Sandberg (audience of 1,000), and Rachel Maddow (audience of 1,200)—have continued to help us grow and diversify our audience.

Of course, none of these events would have been possible without our single-ticket buyers, package subscribers, endowment donors, and George S. Pepper Society members. It should be noted that the more benefits that Pepper Society members receive for the Author Events Series, the greater their membership numbers and their financial contributions to the series. Similarly, author dinners and receptions have continued to be a successful fundraising tool to thank existing Pepper Society members and contributors at various upper echelons. This access also encourages society members to bring new

Figure 1.2. Barack Obama. (Credit: Photo courtesy of the Free Library of Philadelphia Foundation and Kelly & Massa Photography)

donors and corporate representatives to support a wide array of library initiatives, from new programs to the capital campaign.

Finally, as anyone knows who has clicked "contribute" after making an online donation—generally followed with an instant web or e-mail thank you asking for another generous gift—it makes the most sense to actively cultivate one's most committed supporters. For example, earlier this year, the library solicited and received a gift from one of its longtime lecture supporters to endow the position of director of author events, thereby ensuring that the series would continue as a beacon of culture for Philadelphians and the surrounding communities, while living up to the library's mission to advance literacy, guide learning, and inspire curiosity.

CODA

In the end, we did not reinvent the wheel. Author lectures have been taking place since the Greek tragedians and Roman orators addressed their audiences in various fora and continued as Dickens, Twain, and Poe took to the lecture circuit in the 1800s. Fundraising through ticket sales, grants, named endowments, and donor groups has been taking place for the better part of a century. What makes the Free Library of Philadelphia a little different is that with a touch of temerity and some sharp tactical thinking by the Free Library Foundation Development Department, we were able to leverage a combination of community interest, fortunate geography, a strong media market, and foundation and donor support to create and perpetuate a lively series that addresses the needs of cultural consumers in Philadelphia.

ACKNOWLEDGMENTS

Thanks to Elliot Shelkrot, Kathy Gosliner, and Sue Seiter for taking a chance; Sandy Horrocks for guidance; Morris and Ruth Williams for their support; Sara Goddard for her Saraness; and Michelle Sheffer for her copyediting chops.

REFERENCE

McCaffrey, Meg. 2005. "Star Power: Philly's Free Library Has Created a Teen Program That Would Make Oprah Envious." *School Library Journal* 51, no. 1 (January): 48–49.

2

Crazy Smart: Creative Approaches to Developing Your Donor Pipeline and Increasing Support

Thomas B. Hadzor and Kurt H. Cumiskey
Duke University Libraries

OUR ENVIRONMENT

Like many academic research libraries in the United States, the Duke University Libraries receives more philanthropic support from alumni than any other group. Over the past ten years, the percentage of donors to the Libraries who are identified as alumni has held steady at just over 60 percent and is even higher for those giving to the Libraries Annual Fund. But access to this large and supportive group of potential donors (Duke University has over 140,000 living alumni) is problematic. For development purposes at Duke, alumni are "assigned" to the college from which they graduate. Because no one graduates from the Libraries, we cannot solicit alumni until they have given to us. This means our development staff must take creative and untested approaches to attract new donors. We have done that by trying to increase exposure among all demographics, especially alumni, and by taking every opportunity to directly or indirectly make a compelling argument for support. These efforts have, for the most part, been incredibly successful and have given us a new group of best practices to add to an already strong palette of strategies.

Fortunately for our development staff, Duke's university librarian appreciates the importance of raising private money to augment the library budget and encourages development staff to creatively explore all cost-effective fundraising strategies. Without her dedication to the process, we surely would not have seen the significant increases we have. Not only is she fully engaged in closing the largest solicitations, but she is also quick to sign thank-you letters. We believe that good stewardship is paramount to our success and strive to have donors receive a signed thank-you letter within a week of their gift's arrival at Duke.

The development staff comprises the associate university librarian for development, who is responsible for the overall direction of the program, and identifying, cultivating, soliciting, and stewarding all major gift prospects; the assistant director of development, who is responsible for the Annual Fund, planned philanthropy, and corporate and foundation applications; and the development associate, who provides overall support for the department, including generating solicitation and acknowledgment letters, and administering programs like the Friends of the Library and Bookplate Initiative. In addition, the Libraries director of communications, exhibitions coordinator, and graphic designer all work under the development umbrella. While these latter positions support the entire library, positioning them in development has been integral to our recent success.

OUR SUCCESS

As a result of initiatives undertaken by the Libraries in the past few years, the Duke University Libraries has seen substantial increases in the number of donors, cash gifts, and new pledges. Between 2004 and 2013, we have seen an increase in the number of donors to our Annual Fund (unrestricted money used at the discretion of the university librarian) from 827 in 2004 to 1,887 in 2013, and an increase in cash from $287,000 in 2004 to $745,000 in 2013. Increases in the number of overall donors and giving have produced similarly solid numbers, but those—especially cash—fluctuate wildly from year to year because of large pledge payments from foundations and large and unexpected gifts-in-kind. In addition to the Annual Fund, overall giving to the Libraries includes gifts made in support of our building renovation, endowments, gifts-in-kind, and expendable contributions for new or existing initiatives. Figure 2.1 shows the increase in donors over a ten-year period to the Annual Fund (bottom line) and total (top line), while Figure 2.2 shows the increase in giving to the Annual Fund over the same period of time.

In 2010, Duke University Libraries received two transformative gifts. First, David M. Rubenstein, a 1970 Duke University alumnus and member of the university's board of trustees, committed $13.6 million toward the renovation of the Rare Book, Manuscript & Special Collections Library at Duke (in recognition of his generosity, the university's board of trustees renamed the library the David M. Rubenstein Rare Book & Manuscript Library). A few months later, Duke University athletic director Kevin White announced that the Athletics Department would give the Libraries one dollar from every home ticket sporting event. In addition to being generous

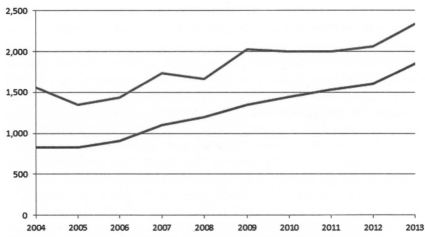

Figure 2.1.   Donors to the Libraries Annual Fund and overall, 2004–2013.

commitments, both gifts gave the Libraries greater exposure. In particular, the Libraries logo and a brief description of the Athletics Library Fund is printed on the back of each ticket. During the next solicitation cycle for our Annual Fund, we anticipated that donors might think all of our needs had been met with these two generous gifts: we made sure to remind them that the Rubenstein gift was designated for a specific purpose (building renovation) and that the Athletics Fund, while unrestricted, did not funnel into the Annual Fund.

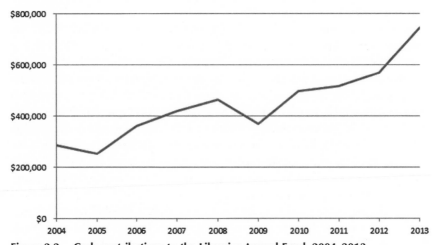

Figure 2.2.   Cash contributions to the Libraries Annual Fund, 2004–2013.

REDOUBLING OUR EFFORTS WITH
RELIABLE STRATEGIES AND BUILDING GOODWILL

Another part of our strategy has been to strengthen already excellent relationships with those people who can make the case for support of the Libraries when we aren't present: library staff, our Library Advisory Board, and our colleagues, especially administrators and generalists, in the university's Central Development Office.

At every opportunity, we remind library colleagues that every one of their interactions with a patron, whether a student, faculty member, researcher, or community patron, reflects on the Libraries. In all staff meetings, we regularly take the opportunity to publicly acknowledge a cash gift received as the result of good public service. A few years ago a parent, whom we're not permitted to solicit, made a gift to the Libraries Annual Fund and included a hand-written note to the university librarian, explaining that she was making the gift because of the help her daughter received as part of our Residence Hall Librarian Program, which is designed to introduce first-year students to services and collections available from the Duke University Libraries. The residence hall librarian serves as an individual point of contact for students throughout their first year at Duke.

Members of our Library Advisory Board are the most generous donors to the Libraries Annual Fund; while they made up less than 0.5 percent of donors in 2013, they gave more than 13 percent toward the total. Just as important, they are more likely than other donors to encourage their friends and classmates to give and are more likely to associate with people who are able to make larger-than-average gifts.

Several years ago, we invited the university's major gifts officers to the Libraries for a tour and lunch. We endeavored to bring to their attention our greatest needs, so if they encountered a donor with an interest in the Libraries, they might match that donor and his or her capacity with the appropriate funding opportunity in the Libraries. A good number of new prospects, both large and small, have come our way as a result. This simple and inexpensive lunch and tour continues to pay substantial dividends, as many major gifts officers regularly talk about the Libraries when they meet with prospects. Major gifts officers and staff of the Alumni Association routinely ask library development staff to give individual tours to alumni who are bringing their children to campus in advance of their application for admission. These alumni, many of whom haven't been back to the library since they graduated, are usually very impressed. Some, in fact, show their gratitude by becoming Libraries donors.

We have taken advantage of those several times each year when our alumni are on campus—Homecoming Weekend, Family Weekend, and Reunion Weekend—to connect with our donors. On these three weekends, we offer two different kinds of tours: a general tour and a behind-the-scenes tour of a department that alumni might find interesting (for instance Data and GIS Services and the consistently popular Conservation Department, which includes a tour of the Digital Production Center). The general tours have been so popular, with more than one hundred alumni registering for each tour, that it's all-hands-on-deck: We divide the registrants into three groups, and development officers take the three groups in different directions. Each tour ends with a "commercial," encouraging alumni for financial support.

Two years ago, the Libraries began hosting a reception for library donors on Reunion Weekend in April. Just after the new year, we send on behalf of the university librarian a printed invitation to all alumni who are in a reunion year (five-year cycle) for a ninety-minute reception in the library in their honor on Friday afternoon. Each year, we've invited nearly 1,000 alumni. Of course, not everyone attends their reunion. But even those who were not planning to attend appreciate being invited to the reception. The receptions have been well attended, with about one hundred people coming on average. The event is staffed by members of the development staff and key senior Libraries administrators. It's a casual event, although the university librarian spends a few minutes to publicly thank those in attendance for their support. People are invited if they've ever made a donation of any size to the Libraries. In many cases, attendees haven't given for several years. But we began receiving gifts from people who were long-lapsed Libraries donors, regardless of whether they attended the reception.

Several years ago, we established two programs specifically to benefit alumni: the Alumni Bookplate Initiative and the Alumni Portal. When an alumnus dies, the Duke Alumni Association (DAA) sends a condolence card to the immediate family. DAA includes with the card a postcard from the Libraries, giving the family the opportunity to help us select a book for the collection in memory of their deceased family member. The Libraries does this free of charge because we think it's the right thing to do. Once a book is selected, the family receives a letter from the university librarian and a copy of the cataloging record showing their family member's name. The university librarian regularly receives letters of appreciation from the families and occasionally cash donations. While the program has not become a large revenue stream, it has generated a tremendous amount of goodwill.

Duke University Libraries has purchased for alumni remote access to more than fifty databases. Statistics show that the databases are getting considerable use, and we are preparing to launch a new marketing campaign for this free service. The initiative has afforded us the opportunity to develop a deeper relationship with the Alumni Association. Alumni also have access to reference librarians through IM, e-mail, or phone contact. We try to convey the message that even though you may have graduated, we want you to continue to think of Duke University Libraries as your library.

That message is one we convey in the acknowledgment letters sent to all Duke seniors who make a gift to the Libraries as part of their senior class gift (on average, about one hundred students a year do so) and to our graduating student workers. It is important to treat our student workers like colleagues when they're students and as our constituency after they've graduated. Several years ago, when we recognized the number of alumni we meet each year who say they worked in the Libraries when they were undergraduates, we thought it was important not only to begin tracking former student workers but also to make them feel extra special upon graduation, to make them understand that their work has contributed to our success. In fact, we didn't realize until he made his generous commitment to the Libraries that David M. Rubenstein, Duke Class of 1970 and member of the university's board of trustees, had worked in the Libraries when he was a student. As the end of each academic year approaches, we invite supervisors to submit the names of all their students who are graduating, whether undergraduate or graduate students. The Libraries recognizes their service in an ad in the student newspaper. We then plan a reception for the graduating student workers and their supervisors before the final exam period. The reception is an opportunity for the university librarian to thank them publicly for their contributions to our success. At the end of the reception, each student receives a small gift and a complimentary one-year membership in the Friends of the Library. We also mark their records in the fundraising database as a student library worker. In this way, we're able to generate lists in the future to keep this group apprised of Libraries developments or to invite them to special events. Since we began recognizing student workers for their contributions to the Libraries, there has been an increase in gifts from this group.

EMBRACING NEW MEDIA

Social media, like Facebook, Twitter, Pinterest, Instagram, Flickr, blogs, and video, has been instrumental in increasing the Libraries' exposure with current and potential donors. When possible, we use tools like Google Analytics to help measure the effectiveness of what we were doing, and we modify our approach if necessary. We post news items on the Libraries Facebook page, and tweet and retweet newsworthy items—for instance, when a student catches his celebrity father reading in the library (see Figure 2.3).

The Libraries main Facebook page has about 1,500 followers, but some of the Libraries departments have more. For instance, University Archives, which is within the David M. Rubenstein Rare Book & Manuscript Library, has 2,000 followers. In February 2012, almost overnight, that number jumped

Figure 2.3. Some students are so impressed that their visiting parents use the Libraries, they tweet about it.

considerably (up from 370). That month, in advance of the UNC-Duke men's basketball game, the archives at UNC and at Duke hosted a contest to see which school could get the most new Facebook followers. The loser had to post a photograph from the winner's digital archives as the profile picture on their site for one week. UNC received more new followers. Even though Duke lost the contest, both institutions won hundreds of new Facebook followers (note: Duke won the basketball game).

We have reconsidered and improved our web presence: By our positioning a Give Now button in the same location on every page, with clear instructions for donors on how to make their gift online by credit card, check, or stock transfer, donors have the opportunity to make a gift anytime and in any way. We never want to be an impediment to someone during their most generous time. Our interactive virtual tour, designed especially for those alumni who have not been back to campus since the renovation and expansion, has been a great opportunity for the Libraries to illustrate how much the facility and services have changed over the years.

In 2009, Duke University Libraries Development, working in concert with the Libraries director of communications, began creating, sending, and posting several videos a year (www.youtube.com/user/DukeUnivLibraries), from a fall and spring solicitation video to short, interesting, and informative videos about events in the Libraries, and then tracked activity (open rate, click-through locations, and so on, using an e-marketing service). It is important to contact donors more frequently than just when we're soliciting them. These videos have generated tremendous interest, which we attribute to several causes. First, we try to keep the videos short, usually less than ninety seconds, because our data show that people tend to stop watching if the message takes too long. Second, we try to make the videos fun, informative, and interesting. We believe that one of the reasons the open rate continues to climb is because the earlier videos were instructional and entertaining.

In our solicitation videos, students or faculty provide fun facts about the Libraries or talk about how the Libraries helped them succeed. An argument for support is much more compelling when it comes from those people who benefit most from our collections and services. And just recently, in an attempt to showcase our highly qualified staff, the solicitation videos have begun featuring Libraries colleagues. For instance, last fall's video showcased the Libraries director of digital scholarship describing a new initiative, Digitize This Book, which allows patrons to request that an out-of-copyright book be scanned by the Libraries Digital Production Center.

To publicize the Libraries new Multimedia Project Studio in the fall of 2012, at the height of the presidential campaign, we challenged Duke students to "be our Super PAC" and make a short mock-election video for the Duke University Libraries. Eligible videos were posted to the Libraries blog and Facebook pages, where we invited people to vote for their favorite. The winning entry, produced and directed by two sophomores, was by far the best solicitation video to date, even better than the videos that were professionally produced. For their creativity and filmmaking skills, the winners received two tickets to the Duke-UNC men's basketball game in Cameron Indoor Stadium on February 13, 2013.

Many of the videos shared with donors are about exciting things happening in the Libraries. Those include a short video on the Friends of the Library Study Break, when members of the Friends of the Library bring home-baked cookies and cakes for students studying during finals week. On what is affectionately called the "Night of 10,000 Cookies," students are often brought to tears with appreciation. Many of them are so stressed from final exams. Home-baked goodies are exactly what they need to get them through finals.

Other videos focus on the Libraries Book Collectors Contest (the winners of the past two contests have gone on to first and second place, respectively, in the national competition); summaries of engaging library programs, exhibitions, or events; and videos of the annual student party. For the past six years, a student organization has planned a party that is held in Perkins Library. While the student organization coordinates the event with Libraries staff, the students raise all the funds and plan and market the event. The Library Party is held each year in late February on a Friday night when the trustees are on campus. The event is attended by several thousand students, faculty, university administrators, and trustees. The Library Party always has a theme based on one of the Libraries' unique special collections. Last year, the party—Heroes and Villains—centered around the Rubenstein Library's outstanding comic book collections, one of the best in the country. Students and staff came dressed as their favorite comic book characters, danced to live and recorded music, and had the opportunity to look at some of our rare first-edition comic books.

We interact with donors and potential donors, including stewardship, using blogs. There are twenty blogs from the Libraries and individual library departments. They are a terrific way for donors to keep abreast of those areas (e.g., conservation) in which they're most interested. At the end of this past fiscal year, the university librarian wrote a thank-you letter to all Libraries donors that listed just some of the things the Libraries accomplished in the past year with their support (with links to blog posts on those projects). She sent the letter via Bronto, an e-mail marketing service that allows analytics tracking. We then posted the letter on the Libraries main blog site so everyone, including non-donors, could read and be inspired to give. Nearly 55 percent of the people who received the initial e-mail opened it, and the university librarian received a number of e-mails from donors pleased with our progress. Furthermore, Bronto allowed us to see that many people clicked on several or all of the stories. Realizing that e-mail doesn't reach everyone, we also sent a postcard that included the web address of the online message.

For several years, we kept track of gifts to the Libraries building project with a spreadsheet and a document that was a series of floor plans. Each time a donor made a gift large enough to name a room or space in recognition of their gift, we would note it in the spreadsheet and modify the document. When meeting with donors outside of the Libraries, major gifts officers or the associate university librarian for development had to carry a copy of the floor plans. Because this was a very cumbersome and time-consuming process, we created an interactive naming opportunities web page that could be accessed by anyone with Internet access: http://library.duke.edu/support/naming/opportunities/ (see Figure 2.4). The success of the naming opportunities site was immediate and overwhelming. Within a day of the site going live, we secured a $100,000 commitment.

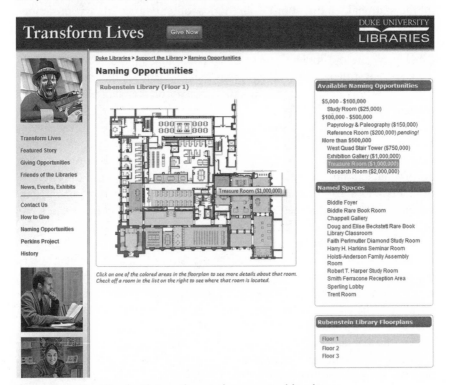

Figure 2.4. The Libraries' interactive naming opportunities site.

The site allows a donor to navigate the library by floor and price range. Named spaces are blue and available spaces are green. When a potential donor goes to the menu of available spaces and hovers over a $25,000 room, for instance, that space will become a brighter color on the map. If the potential donor clicks on the room, a box pops up with images or renderings of the space. When one of our development officers is meeting with donors, they can easily reference the site. The site has gotten considerable attention from colleagues on campus—especially those who are beginning or in the middle of a capital project—and nationally. Because we designed, built, and administer the site in-house for a fraction of the cost of having it produced by an external vendor, talking about the site gives us the opportunity to explain the benefits of identifying talented staff and negotiating for them to help with our fundraising program.

THE OVERLOOKED AND IMMEASURABLE IMPACT OF PRINT MEDIA

In the rush to embrace new media, we occasionally forget the tremendous impact of print media, including postcards, advertisements, magazines, and newsletters. A large percentage of our donor base still prefers print media, and even those who prefer to be solicited by e-mail and to donate online like to have a hard-copy of the Libraries magazine. It may be in vogue to cut budgets for magazines, but we have found that they give us the best opportunity to steward our donors and attract new donors.

We solicited feedback from donors and found that most of them want to receive the Friends of the Library newsletter electronically (though we still print and mail it to about 300 donors) but want to receive a copy of the biannual *Duke Libraries* magazine by mail. Both the newsletter and the magazine are given to anyone who has made a gift of at least $50 over the previous year. Digital versions of the magazine are available on the Libraries website.

We found that, over time, too many donors lapsed because they'd missed a year of giving and then no longer received the magazine. In short, the Libraries fell off their radar. By finding a less expensive printer, we were able to increase the number of magazines we ordered for the same price, and now we send them to donors who've made a gift of at least $50 during the past three years. What we found is that a good number of lapsed donors began giving again.

Each magazine issue is filled with newsworthy articles about Libraries activities. The director of communications, who is responsible for producing the magazine, tries to run at least one article in each issue about a different way donors have made a difference. One such story was about an alumna who made a gift of $5,000 to the Libraries renovation project. As a way to recognize her gift, the Libraries gave her the opportunity to name a study carrel, a small office within the library assigned to a faculty member or graduate student for a year. When she made the gift, she told us it was in honor of seven friends who had remained close since their freshman year at Duke. They were all turning fifty that year. The plaque we had fabricated and mounted outside the study carrel listed their eight names and said, "In celebration of friendship and 400 fabulous years." Other development articles have highlighted donors who've made planned gifts, who've made modest gifts in the Honoring with Books Program, or who've created an endowment to support a position or collection.

Beginning in 2009, we increased the Libraries exposure with our largest donor group (alumni) by running a full-page advertisement in each issue of *Duke Magazine*, published five times a year and sent to all living alumni and select other university supporters. Because of the restrictions on whom we can solicit, the ads are one of the only ways we can get in front of the entire alumni base. In the first two years, the ads, which used the theme "Transform Lives," attempted to speak to different demographics (e.g., alumni, parents, community patrons, students, faculty). Each ad included a large, colorful image of a Libraries supporter, with his or her connection to the Libraries, and a provocative quote. At the bottom of the ad, readers were encouraged to go to a unique URL for the rest of the story. Google Analytics informed us that in the two weeks following each publication, we had a tremendous spike in activity on our website (see Figure 2.5). For instance, in the first week of October 2010, visits to the Libraries development site jumped from near nothing to about 150 views. Visitors stayed on average just over one minute, or about thirty seconds less than those who visited other pages on the site. After the initial flush of excitement generated by the ads, website activity settled down to just a few visits each day. Despite the relatively modest number of people visiting the development website as a result of the ads, in the first full year we received $130,000 in new commitments from alumni who were giving to the Libraries for the first time!

After two years, we wanted to create ads that were more dynamic so we took a different approach. The new ads (dubbed Crazy Smart) focused on different library initiatives (e.g., Digitize This Book), collections (e.g., digitization of the entire run of the student newspaper from the 1960s), and services (e.g., the Residence Hall Librarian Program) rather than on attempting to attract a different demographic. Whereas the ads in the first two years had a flat green background, the new ads have had provocative images and catchy text. For this series of ads, according to Google Analytics, there have been nearly twice as many visitors in the two weeks immediately following each issue publication (see Figure 2.6). Even more important, visitors stayed for

Google Analytics

Go to this report

http://library.duke.edu - http://library.duke.edu
A-library.duke.edu

Content Drilldown

Jun 1, 2010 - Jun 30, 2011

ALL » PAGE PATH LEVEL 1: /support/ » PAGE PATH LEVEL 2: /story/

All Visits
0.01%

Explorer

Page path level 3		Pageviews	Unique Pageviews	Avg. Time on Page	Bounce Rate	% Exit
		2,022 % of Total: 0.01% (15,253,935)	1,491 % of Total: 0.01% (11,574,613)	00:01:06 Site Avg: 00:01:28 (-25.61%)	73.86% Site Avg: 61.54% (20.02%)	40.21% Site Avg: 41.00% (-1.92%)
1.	/archive/	**1,149**	884	00:01:08	82.82%	46.21%
2.	/index.html	**873**	607	00:01:03	58.74%	32.30%

Rows 1 - 2 of 2

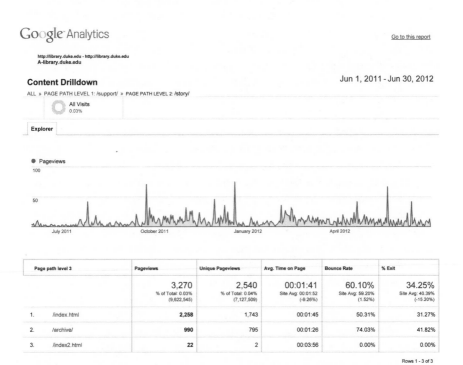

Figure 2.5. After a pronounced spike in interest immediately following Transform Lives advertisements, activity returns to normal.

Google Analytics

Go to this report

http://library.duke.edu - http://library.duke.edu
A-library.duke.edu

Content Drilldown

Jun 1, 2011 - Jun 30, 2012

ALL » PAGE PATH LEVEL 1: /support/ » PAGE PATH LEVEL 2: /story/

All Visits
0.03%

Explorer

Page path level 3		Pageviews	Unique Pageviews	Avg. Time on Page	Bounce Rate	% Exit
		3,270 % of Total: 0.03% (9,622,545)	2,540 % of Total: 0.04% (7,127,509)	00:01:41 Site Avg: 00:01:52 (-9.26%)	60.10% Site Avg: 59.20% (1.52%)	34.25% Site Avg: 40.39% (-15.20%)
1.	/index.html	**2,258**	1,743	00:01:45	50.31%	31.27%
2.	/archive/	**990**	795	00:01:26	74.03%	41.82%
3.	/index2.html	**22**	2	00:03:56	0.00%	0.00%

Rows 1 - 3 of 3

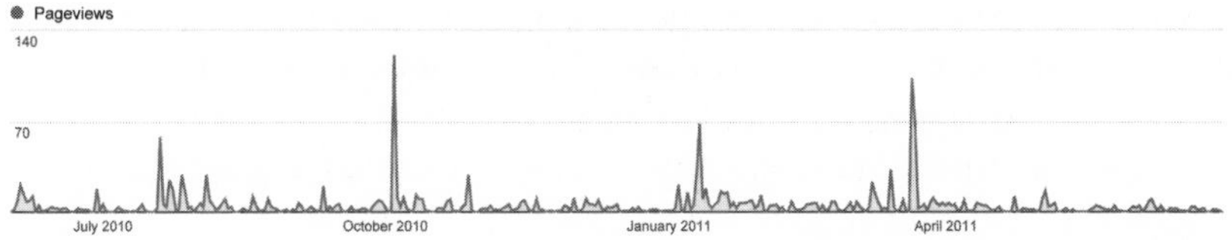

Figure 2.6. Interest among alumni greatly increases following Crazy Smart advertisements, but remains high afterward.

nearly twice as long and, when finished, visited other pages on the Libraries development site (most notably, the pages having to do with the Libraries renovation project, and the page on how to become a Friend of the Library). Best of all, the activity on the Libraries website between issues of *Duke Magazine* dropped much less than it did during the run of the first ads. More people were visiting the development web pages, they were staying longer, and they were looking at things they had not originally gone there for. The ads were producing the outcome we hoped for. View the entire set of Crazy Smart ads from the Libraries' Flickr account at www.flickr.com/photos/duke univlibraries/ (see Figure 2.7).

CONCLUSION

As competition for philanthropic dollars increases, it is imperative to try new measures to make a compelling argument for support, to enlist the assistance of qualified people who also can advocate for support, and to familiarize yourself with those donors most able and inclined to support your library. Because alumni make up the largest portion of our donors, and because we are greatly restricted in soliciting them, we have advertised in the alumni magazine, provided free database access for alumni, shared information about the Libraries without soliciting them, and taken every opportunity to meet with them on campus. We have determined that these are not only best practices but also outstanding practices because they have been neither expensive nor time consuming to implement. Furthermore, they could be tried at a wide array of libraries. For the long-term financial health of Duke University Libraries, we have put considerable focus on building the pipeline, and, in the past ten years, we have more than doubled the number of donors to our Annual Fund. We know a high percentage of major donors today began their support by making modest gifts to the Libraries.

We continue to review the literature, attend conferences and workshops, and speak with colleagues across the country, looking for new ways to build our pipeline. For instance, we planned an event in New York City for young alumni in February 2014. The casual cocktail event featured a short "commercial" from the university librarian. A board member generously provided the venue and underwrote the event, so the cost to the Libraries was minimal.

It is almost impossible to draw a direct link between a new initiative and increased fundraising (donors and dollars). We have not run a campaign with a coded brochure that would allow us to know precisely if there was a connection. In fact, such campaigns in our experience are not as effective. We know it's unlikely that a donor will see our ad in the *Duke Magazine*,

Figure 2.7. Advertisement in *Duke Magazine* announcing the Athletics Department's Library Fund.

go to our website, and immediately make a gift. It happens sometimes, but not frequently. Much more likely is that, over time, after seeing several ads, after talking with classmates about where they give, after attending a Duke football or basketball game and seeing our logo on the back of their ticket, after walking across campus and seeing someone carrying a Duke University Libraries canvas bag or umbrella, or after attending one of our tours when they've returned to campus for Reunion Weekend, they make their first gift to the Libraries. Successful fundraising, including building the pipeline, is the result of many different kinds of approaches over many years. We're patient and have confidence that, once our message is communicated, potential donors, especially alumni, will support the Libraries.

3

Selling Used Books to Generate Library Funds

JANE RUTLEDGE
Friends of the Tippecanoe County Public Library

TIPPECANOE COUNTY PUBLIC LIBRARY BOOK SALE

"Our book sale is the engine that powers our Friends group." That's the statement made several years ago by a former president of Friends of the Tippecanoe County Public Library in Lafayette, Indiana, and it is still true today. Our quarterly book sales are our largest source of income and bring in most of our new members, as well as being the project that pulls together many volunteers in a team effort and brings us positive publicity in the community. Selling used books is the signature fundraiser for many, probably most, public library Friends groups. It fits right in with a library's mission, and it appeals to our target group: people who appreciate and support reading, books, and libraries.

Last-Minute Preparations and Presale

Four times a year, a line begins to form outside our downtown library by mid-afternoon on a Friday. The early arrivals are the book dealers, who bring boxes, bags, and sometimes even lawn chairs in order to be among the first to enter the library when the members-only presale begins at 7:30 p.m. By the time the doors open, the line will usually extend all the way down the length of the building (see Figure 3.1). Friends members have the passes that were mailed out with the newsletter ten days earlier, and we also advertise that we will accept new memberships at the sale.

Meanwhile, inside the building, as soon as the library doors have closed at 6:00 p.m., about fifteen to twenty volunteers begin working rapidly, setting up thirty-five tables in the library's large lobby areas and filling them with boxes of books. The previous evening has already been devoted to shuttling

35

Jane Rutledge

Figure 3.1. Friends of the Tippecanoe County Public Library line up for the members-only presale. (Credit: Photograph by Larry French)

boxes of books from our storage building across the street and setting up and stocking another thirty-five tables in the meeting room. Books, CDs, DVDs, videotapes, magazines, and puzzles are moved up from our basement work area. Cashboxes have been readied with starting change, and the volunteers' nametags are set out for pickup in a library conference room. Membership forms and an up-to-date membership list are on a table near the entrance where the membership chair will sign up new members—usually twenty to thirty at each sale. The small kitchen by the meeting room is stocked with snacks and drinks for the volunteers.

At about 7:00 p.m., the next set of volunteers—the cashiers and floaters—arrive, don their blue aprons, and find their nametags. The setup is finished just in time for the workers to have a slice of pizza and a few minutes of early shopping before the doors open at 7:30 p.m. The library director and a Friends officer greet shoppers at the door, collecting their passes and sending those without passes to the membership table. Once again, we've managed to launch our Big Book Sale.

During the sale, there will usually be two cashier tables with two workers at each one; for the presale we have eight cashiers working. In addition, for the presale only, one end of the circulation desk is used as the "Large Order" holding area where customers buying large numbers of items may leave their purchases until they are ready to check out. Three volunteers work there, labeling boxes and bags with the buyers' names and adding up the prices. At least three more volunteers work as "floaters," keeping the tables neat, answering questions, and reminding people that stacks, bags, and boxes of books cannot be stashed in corners or under tables but must be taken to "Large Orders," where they will be labeled and counted. Because the books are placed on the tables in shallow boxes, spines up, it is easy to keep the tables neat by consolidating boxes as they begin to empty. The floaters also watch for books that end up out of place and return them to the correct categories so that the sale stays as organized as we can make it.

By closing time at 9:30 p.m., the crowd has thinned, and there are empty spaces on the tables and a few emptied boxes waiting to be gathered up and taken back to our downstairs work area. When the door closes, the counting crew, usually two or three people and the Friends treasurer, gather up the cashboxes and settle down in a secure area to count the money. While they prepare the cashboxes for the next day and make up deposit slips, the book-sale chair and one or two helpers do a final check of the tables, sometimes even counting the boxes in each category to compare with our starting count. When the cashboxes and the prepared deposits are safely locked up, the last official act of the evening is the presentation of the day's total to the book-sale chair. In two hours, we will have taken in about $7,000, about 40 percent of our eventual total.

The Three-Day Sale

The sale continues on Saturday from 9:00 a.m. to 6:00 p.m., with cashiers and floaters working three-hour shifts (see Figure 3.2). On Sunday, all items are half-price, and the hours are 1:00 p.m. to 6:00 p.m. At about 4:00 p.m. on Sunday, the Sunday Shuffle crew and the floaters begin shifting all the remaining stock from the lobby areas into the meeting room so that by closing

Figure 3.2.   Shoppers at the book sale. (Credit: Photograph by Larry French)

time on Sunday the book sale is out of the main library area and the week begins with the library back in order. Money is counted at intervals throughout the sale, and after closing for the day, the new total is announced in an e-mail to Friends officers and sale workers.

Monday is the last day of the book sale, and from 9:00 a.m. to 3:00 p.m. everything remaining is up for grabs at only $2 a bag. It's a busy day, beginning with handing out grocery bags to the early comers waiting for the doors to open. As the tables begin to empty, floaters continue to consolidate and empty boxes; as categories sell out, their signs are taken down. By about noon there will be a few empty tables on which boxes can be stacked and signs organized for storage. At 3:00 p.m. we make a final count of the number of boxes remaining (usually fewer than 10 percent of what we started with) and begin stacking the books and returning boxes to our sorting area. By about 4:00 p.m. our boxes and signs are all stored and the remaining books are ready for their new owner. Before the sale we try to find someone who will agree to buy our leftovers, supplying his own boxes and labor and taking everything, so when the books have been picked up, the only remaining task is to return the tables to our storage building—and, of course, to e-mail the final sale total, usually between $16,000 and $18,000, to the book sale crew, with a big "Thanks, everybody" for making it happen again.

At Tippecanoe County Public Library, we do this four times a year. In addition, we maintain an active program of online book sales that brings in another $16,000–$18,000 annually, so we are able to fund lots of programs at the library; support summer reading clubs; treat the library staff to a holiday dinner and to food at staff meetings and special events; support a scholarship program; pay for the printing and mailing of the library's newsletter; purchase special equipment; and make large contributions to capital campaigns for new branches and renovations.

Of course, an ongoing project of this magnitude did not happen overnight. Our Friends group is celebrating its fiftieth anniversary, and our archives are full of accounts of book sales, beginning with one table of donated books and growing and changing through the years. We finally settled into our pattern of four sales a year about fifteen years ago, and we keep finding ways to make improvements to our systems.

BEST PRACTICES AND TIPS FOR BOOK SALES

Donations

While a large number of the books we sell are library withdrawals, most of our stock comes to us from community donations. People need to know what you will accept and how to get it to you. Our big "Donations Are Now Being Accepted" poster goes up in the library lobby immediately after each sale. We mention books, DVDs and CDs, video tapes, and puzzles, and we say, "No Magazines, Please." When people inquire about donating records, we suggest that they take them to our neighboring library in West Lafayette, Indiana, where the Friends have a big record sale annually. If records show up in our donations, we call the West Lafayette Friends, and one of their volunteers comes by and picks them up. We still do receive magazines from time to time, and a few of them even make their way into the sale (usually specialized cooking, needlework, hobby, and art publications).

When people call asking if we will accept whatever it is that they have, we try to say yes. We do explain that whatever we feel we can't sell we will probably put out on our Free Cart in the outer lobby.

It needs to be easy for people to donate. Our publicity states that donations can be brought to the downtown library during regular library hours, and we also provide a telephone number to call if donors need help transporting their books. Two of our volunteers enjoy going after books, and we have received some very nice donations that might not have come our way if we had not provided some help. When our circulation area was renovated a few years ago, space was set aside and enclosed for Friends donations. We have two book carts in the donation closet for staff to leave the books on, and a Friends volunteer empties them daily. Large donations can also be brought to the loading dock at the back of the building.

We have other ways to spread the word: the library newsletter, the Friends newsletter, the library's web page, social media, posters, bookmarks, and fly-ers handed out to the sellers at garage sales suggesting that leftover books be donated. We include with every appeal (1) what we want, (2) where and when to bring it, and (3) how to get in touch with us.

Books given to the Friends are considered charitable donations by the IRS. Not everyone wants a receipt, but receipts do need to be available for those who do. We use a receipt developed by our library; the forms are available at the circulation desk, and on occasion we have also mailed them to donors. We do not attempt to put a dollar figure on donations; the form simply shows what was donated, such as "Two boxes of books."

The Sorting Process

Sad to say, we need to throw some things away. Books that have been wet, moldy books, books that have been chewed on, books with a strong odor—all of these simply have to be discarded. We also discard videotapes and other media that are home-recorded, as well as books that are seriously damaged, missing pages, falling apart, or defaced by lots of writing and underlining.

Then there are the items that we know from long experience simply will not sell at our sale: encyclopedias more than ten years old, encyclopedia yearbooks, condensed books, most magazines, out-of-date (but not yet collectible) almanacs, many old textbooks, very worn paperbacks, incomplete sets, and odd volumes. These usually go out in the library lobby on our Free Cart, and many of them will be carried away to new homes. Every couple of days, any items remaining on the free cart are discarded to make room for the next batch.

As we unpack donations, dusty books get wiped off, old price stickers are removed (a palette knife is a great tool for this), and really ragged dust jackets may be discarded. We pride ourselves on presenting an attractive sale.

Those items that remain when we've dealt with the rejects are priced by the sorting room managers and stacked on tables and carts for the sorting crews to distribute into their proper categories. We sort weekly, with an afternoon crew and an evening crew alternating weeks. Sorters get a reminder e-mail a few days before their sorting shift. We maintain an informal and very sociable atmosphere in the sorting room so that volunteers enjoy coming back. An annual luncheon for the sorters is a nice thank-you and an opportunity to get better acquainted.

Sharing with the Library

Depending on your local circumstances, the library itself may be able to use some of your donations. One neighboring library has a holding table in their sorting area where library staff look over all of the incoming donations before the Friends begin sorting them. Other libraries have wish lists that are posted in the sorting area. When local high school yearbooks are donated, we always check to see if the library still needs them for their collection, and one staff member periodically sorts through our DVDs as she develops a back-up collection of heavily used titles. We consider these items a direct service to the library and usually mention them in our annual report.

Pricing

The usual system for Friends book sales is to set base prices for books and other items. A common pattern is one price for mass-market paperbacks, a slightly higher price for large-format (called "trade") paperbacks, and about twice that price for hardcover books. Magazines are often about half the price of mass-market paperbacks. Videotapes are now often about the same price as a mass-market paperback; CDs and DVDs are hardcover prices or higher. Children's books are often half the price of adult books.

However, there will always be exceptional items that could be priced higher, and items that don't fall easily into those categories. You'll need to develop a marking system for those.

Our preference for marking prices is the use of round, removable stickers, often called "color-coding labels," that we buy in large quantities when we find a good price for them. It's important to use the removable and not the permanent ones. We use only green, and we print prices on them with our office printer. Our prices for special items are in whole dollars to make counting and adding easier for our cashiers. On books, the stickers go on the front cover, upper left, where they are easy to spot as you lift a book out of the box.

Deciding on prices is a subjective process. We price books in excellent condition a dollar or two higher than the usual price, and we also raise prices on books that are in sought-after categories or are hard to find. Art books, books on the Civil War, books about Native Americans, and books of local interest, for instance, may be priced higher even if not in excellent condition. An author's autograph in the book also raises the price, and we add a green "signed" sticker under the price sticker. Our base price for a hardcover book is currently $2, and we rarely have anything in the sale priced over $6.

Some Friends groups keep their specially priced items separate from the rest of the sale books, but we sort ours into their categories along with the unpriced items. (Exceptions: our Practically Perfect fiction category, and the Gift Quality books at our December sale.) Our base prices are posted at the sale, and the most effective way we have found is to print them right on the category signs. We also put price stickers on any items that might confuse the cashiers—magazines that look like paperback books, for instance.

Our prices are firm: we do not negotiate any prices for any reason. Because we have a half-price day and a "Bag Day," anyone who feels our prices are too high can return later for a better deal. Our cleanup at the end of every sale day ensures that customers cannot successfully stash books to pick up the next day at a reduced price. By the way, any complaint that a price is too high can be answered, with a friendly smile, "Well, it's all for the library."

Our final day clears out a lot of items at $2 for a bag. We supply the bags, which we purchase in quantity from a local supermarket. Bag Day prices vary; we've seen as high as $8 a bag. One Friends group offers two options: $1 for a small plastic bag, and $2 for a regular grocery bag. We've also seen other methods, such as selling by weight or by the inch.

Sorting and Boxing

Because our sales are large (we estimate about 25,000 items per sale), we sort books into lots of categories to make shopping easier for our customers. At our weekly sorting sessions we sort into about sixty-five categories—some large (Romance, for instance) and others quite specialized (Genealogy, Agriculture). The more categories, of course, the more sorting space you will need.

Sometimes we are stumped, and an item goes into the Hard-to-Classify category. Another catch-all category is Old, where pre-1970 books of all sorts are likely to end up. Here's where we also put the odds and ends—a newspaper announcing the Kennedy assassination, sports media guides from past years, souvenir programs from special events, and so forth. These items get price stickers, often just $0.25 or $0.50, and are stacked in shallow boxes.

Books are packed into open boxes, spines up, titles all facing the same direction. A few years ago we began purchasing boxes so that we now have standard sizes; we reclaim them as they empty at the sale and reuse them until they begin to wear out. Mass-market paperbacks fit nicely into soft-drink flats. We cut boxes to 4 1/2 and 5 1/2-inch depths for most books, and we use smaller, deeper boxes for larger books. Of course, scavenged boxes are quite usable when cut down to the needed depth.

Children's large-format picture books are packed in small boxes that we cut down with slanted sides. They are packed standing up with the covers showing so that browsers can easily flip through the books and see all the titles. Magazines are conveniently displayed in that style of box as well.

We keep a tally sheet of filled boxes to make it easier to organize the sale layout.

Organizing the Sale

We like to keep similar topics together, and our layout is as consistent as we can make it, with categories in the same general areas sale after sale. Children's books are always in the main lobby, and fiction categories in the north lobby, with nonfiction and media in the meeting room. The first tables you see as you enter the main lobby will probably hold our Practically Perfect fiction and coffee-table books, as well as any categories we are highlighting at that sale.

Some Friends have sale venues complete with shelves, but all of our sale books are on tables. Aisles between tables need to be as wide as you can manage to make them, with three feet an absolute minimum, and they need to be straight, with no dead ends. Every space is different, but the main things to consider are traffic flow and access to emergency exits.

Our tables are full at the beginning of a sale, and we try to minimize the number of overflow boxes, which end up on the floor under the tables. We sometimes hold back books for the next sale; two or three boxes under a table are enough to contribute to congestion at a sale. One goal of the floaters is to get any floor boxes onto the tables as soon as space becomes available. If you must have boxes on the floor, paperbacks are going to be easiest to handle.

Bag Day at the end of the sale presents its own logistical problems, as many buyers will want to purchase multiple bags and we no longer have a holding area available. For this part of the sale, we allow customers to stash filled bags under the sale tables until they are ready to check out, and we provide slips of paper and markers so they can label their bags.

Signage is important in making the sale buyer-friendly. Categories need clear, easy-to-read signs, and if your venue is spread out or cut up into separate areas, you may need directional signs to help people get to what they're looking for. We also have "Do NOT Stack Books Here" signs posted in every tempting bare space and corner, and a few signs outlining our book prices. We have learned, though, that printing the pricing system on each category sign is the most effective way to communicate that message.

There needs to be a go-to person for questions that arise during the sale. In our case, it's the book sale chair, or the person to whom he or she has handed off the responsibility. Everyone helping at the sale needs to know who's in charge at the moment. We are fortunate that our library director spends a lot of time at the sale too. If your sale is on library property, be sure you have a staff member available for anything that becomes an issue of library policy or property.

Publicity

It's clear that the success of a sale depends on how many people actually come through the doors looking for books; one of our past presidents called it the "buyer-to-book ratio." Brainstorm all the possibilities: posters in the library; posters in places around town where likely customers will see them (near colleges and in coffee shops, as well as supermarkets and community centers); press releases to all the local and area media; public service announcements to radio and television stations; community bulletin boards (both physical and online); and all the social media you have access to. Your library's newsletter and website will, of course, highlight the sale, and if your Friends group has a Facebook page, it's a great way to remind interested people of the upcoming sale.

Reaching further afield, there are also websites devoted to advertising used-book sales. The best we've used is booksalefinder.com, which provides free notices for Friends groups. Book dealers and collectors do check those sites, and you may attract some visitors from outside your immediate community.

Another publicity effort is cheap and easy: bookmarks. We print them on plain paper five to a page, with the Friends logo, book sale dates and times, and of course the location. They are available in the library for about a month before the sale, and we sometimes take handfuls to distribute to book groups or other interested organizations. At the book sale, the cashiers give each person a bookmark with the dates of the next sale.

Volunteers

No doubt about it—a successful book sale is a lot of work and requires a lot of people. The good news is that volunteering at the Friends book sale can be a lot of fun.

Twenty-five years ago, when the small book sales at our library began to grow in size and duration, the Friends officers realized they could not do it all by themselves. One officer sat down with the Friends membership list (about eighty families at the time) and called everyone, looking for cashiers, floaters, and help setting up. She was surprised and pleased to find a dozen people who said yes to helping at the sale and another dozen or so who said they'd like to be called for a future sale. She immediately started some of the systems we still use today: Volunteers check in on arrival, receive a nametag, are introduced to their fellow workers, are welcomed by the book sale chair or the person in charge, and are given a quick introduction to their job. By now, we are able to pair up new volunteers with old-timers who can show them the ropes. She also made sure that everyone knew that there were drinks and snacks available in the meeting room kitchen. When the shift ended and new volunteers arrived, she asked the departing volunteers to return their name-tags for future use and asked if they'd be willing for us to call them again.

We provide a locked room for volunteers' coats and bags; the sale chairman and the person in charge are the only ones with keys.

The sale keeps growing and so do our volunteer needs, but we have been able to keep up. Our membership forms have boxes to check for volunteer interests, and the book sale recruiter calls everyone who checks the box for book sales. He sends out a volunteer appeal by e-mail about three weeks before the sale, asking volunteers to sign up for their preferred shifts. A follow-up e-mail about a week later lets people who haven't yet responded see what openings remain, and a few phone calls suffice to fill up the list.

For most Friends groups, the hardest volunteer slots to fill are those that involve heavy lifting. For setup, many groups rely on outside help—service groups, Boy Scouts, athletic teams, fraternity (and sorority) pledge classes, and sometimes people working off their community service hours for the court system. Some of these alternatives require appropriate paperwork, and all require effective supervision.

Book Dealers

Some of our best customers are book dealers, and we would be reluctant to try to discourage them from coming. Some Friends groups have banned the use of handheld barcode scanners (used by booksellers for checking online prices) in an attempt to keep the sale fair and orderly. We have not done so, but we do insist on courteous behavior and absolutely no hoarding—we do not allow anyone to stash large quantities of books and sort through them later. Most of the dealers pay their dues and come to the members-only presale, when our "Large Order" area is available for holding the books they've chosen. The presence of floaters and book sale committee members in all the sale areas helps to keep the sale courteous, and our library director is very willing to confront anyone acting unacceptably. It's easy to establish the ground rules with dealers; most of them will be at the very front of the line on presale night and can be informed before the doors open, in a friendly manner, of the hoarding ban and the location of the "Large Order" area (see Figure 3.3).

We welcome dealers as members but do not allow dealers to work in the sorting room, and we do not allow them to assist with sale setup.

Figure 3.3.   The "Large Order" area in action. (Credit: Photograph by Larry French)

Managing the Money

It's really important to establish secure systems for handling the money for an event of this scope. Our ground rules are quite simple: No one handles money alone, and money does not sit around uncounted. We have six cash boxes for the sale and all are stocked with the same amount of opening change; usually two or three are in use at a time. We have scheduled counting times throughout the sale, based on our experience of when the boxes begin to be uncomfortably full, and at the end of each day. The counting crew begins by exchanging the reserve cashboxes for the active ones, and then retires to a secure room to restock the boxes with opening change for the next use. The rest of the money from the boxes is counted, the checks stamped for deposit, and deposit slips filled out. Everything is counted twice and by two different people; the refilled boxes are double-checked, the checks are added up, and that total added again. Checks are listed on the deposit slips with the last name of the person on the check. Because our deposit slips have room for only seventeen names, we may have several deposits from one counting period. The carbon copy from the deposit slip is marked with the deposit number. A cash form listing the paper money in each deposit is filled out and initialed by two counters. We do not bother to count coins as the sale goes on; we take them to the bank for counting at the end of the sale.

Deposits ready for the bank are sealed in bank deposit bags so that once a deposit is counted and recorded, it cannot be tampered with. The treasurer has a notebook with a page for each day of the sale in which deposits are recorded, and the deposit-slip carbons, cash forms, and adding machine tapes are stapled together and kept in a large envelope with the notebook. At the end of the sale, a separate deposit is made up in the amount of the beginning change, which makes the bookkeeping easier for us. This system has made errors in bank deposits extremely rare, ensures proper handling of the money, and also provides a daily total of actual income. We find that our volunteers and our library staff are always eager to hear the running total.

We do accept checks, and we are able to accept credit cards through our library's credit card system. For a credit card purchase, the cashier adds up the customer's bill and gives him a small form with the total to take to the designated staff member at the circulation desk. The books stay at the cashier's table until the customer returns and shows his credit card receipt to claim them. At the end of each sale day, a staff member collects the Friends credit card sales information and provides us with a total. From a recent discussion on the United for Libraries electronic discussion group, we learned that a number of Friends groups have begun to accept credit cards through an electronic device that can be plugged into a cell phone or tablet.

Sales tax rules will vary, depending on your state and local taxation systems, so it's important to check with the taxing authorities in your own location. A few enlightened states have waived sales taxes for library support groups selling donated books.

Leftovers

We minimize our leftovers by weeding out the obvious during the sorting process, but there will always be books left over, even after a day at half price and another day at $2 a bag. Our sale chair tries to find a buyer for the leftovers ahead of time, and if we don't find a buyer, we may find another nonprofit willing to take them away. We require that the recipient of the leftovers take everything, in their own boxes and with their own labor, and within a few hours after our final close. If we end up with only fifteen or twenty boxes and no one to take them, we can store them and put them out on the Free Cart over the next few weeks.

There are a few companies that make a business out of book sale leftovers. Often they require that you ship the books to them, and sometimes the promise is that they'll sell the books online and send you a percentage of the profit. We suggest that you check out any such offer by asking around to see if other libraries or Friends groups have dealt with them and what their experience has been.

Celebrating Success

Everyone likes to be part of a success story, so we try to celebrate our successes with thank-yous to everyone who helps. We'll often have pictures up on our Facebook page (www.facebook.com/friendsoftcpl) along with messages from the president and the book sale chair in appreciation of everyone who donated, sorted, organized, worked, and bought books. Another nice touch is sending a postcard to all the sale volunteers with the grand total and a big "Thanks for making it happen!"

Several years ago we began presenting small lapel pins to our volunteers every year. The design remains the same, but the color changes from year to year. We hand them out at the book sale, and the volunteers have begun putting them on their sale nametags. You can spot the "old hands"—some people have eight or nine pins on their nametags—and it contributes to the team spirit that we hope to encourage.

MAKING THE MOST OF SPECIAL DONATIONS

Sorting through the donations is a treasure hunt of sorts, and sometimes treasures emerge. Many Friends groups have found ways to market and sell their more valuable items for prices higher than they can expect to get at the regular used-book sale.

Silent Auction

For several years our book sale featured a silent auction area: three tables with special books displayed where customers could submit sealed bids. It was a great way to make a bit of extra income, and it was a way to spotlight antiquarian books, books of local lore and history, fine illustrated editions (such as Easton Press and Folio Society books), collectible first editions and signed copies, and sometimes just the out of the ordinary. At one sale, for instance, an auction item that drew a lot of attention was the Outhouse Collection—an assortment of books, photographs, and postcards on the topic of outhouses, ranging from the serious to the silly.

Space considerations led us to abandon silent auctions at the book sale, but we do still feature a silent auction as part of our Friends annual meeting. Other Friends groups have books on display for a month at a time in the library, with bids recorded in a notebook at the circulation desk, and another has made a large book-and-basket auction into their main fundraiser.

Online Sales

We continue to receive donations of very specialized and technical books (ours is an academic community), antiquarian items, books that would be of local interest in other localities, the occasional fine edition, high school and college yearbooks from other states, and sometimes just unusual items. Back in 2001, a member with experience on eBay suggested that we try selling some of our special items online, and she offered to help us set up an account and get started. We accepted her offer, and now we sell books on both Amazon and eBay. It's a great way to find homes for very special items, and our annual online sales income is about the equivalent of one of our regular book sales.

A few tips for selling online: First, go where the buyers are. At the moment, the sites with the most traffic are Amazon and eBay, and that's where we list our books.

Used books can be listed on Amazon, but only if a catalog page already exists that matches your item exactly: title, author, format (hardcover, paperback), edition, and year. Just about anything—books, back issues of magazines, postcards, and so on—can be listed on eBay, but it's more labor intensive, as you must upload a picture and write your own description.

When your book sells on Amazon, payment is almost automatic: Amazon collects payment from the buyer, deducts its fees, and credits the rest to your seller account. Every two weeks, your bank receives your income as a direct deposit. When you sell on eBay, the seller pays you directly, usually via Pay-Pal, and eBay bills you for its fees monthly.

Selling online requires a few consistent volunteers. Once you have set up shop online, your account and your e-mail must be monitored at least daily, and items need to be shipped promptly. Setting up all of your online accounts (Amazon, eBay, PayPal) requires credit card and bank information. You need a way to take pictures if you're listing on eBay (we use a flat-bed scanner), and you need storage space for your online items and a system of keeping track so you can find an item when it sells. Books must be packaged carefully and securely for mailing and shipped right away.

There is a learning curve, so you'll need to do some homework. Read listings for used books to see how other people describe them, and take some time to learn the language of editions, printings, bindings, and various flaws. The large book sale sites that search a number of venues (bookfinder.com is one we like) are useful in doing your market research and deciding on prices.

Any site that allows you to list items for sale will have rules, procedures, and policies, and it's vitally important to read them all and follow them carefully. The seller discussion forums associated with the sites can give you helpful tips and alert you to the common errors that sellers make.

The most economical way to ship books is by the United States Post Office's media-mail rate. Their website at www.usps.com provides lots of information on rates, services, and restrictions, and when in doubt your local post office can be very helpful. There are several online programs available for purchasing postage and printing your mailing labels; fees and service vary, of course, but again the online discussions can help you make an informed decision.

If you don't want to take on all the details yourself, you may be able to reap some of the benefits of selling online by finding a local seller who will sell online on your behalf for a share of the profits.

We have enjoyed selling online. It's fun to see what people buy, and it has expanded the range of items we can find homes for. College and high school yearbooks do much better online than at the local sale, and we sometimes get messages that make us smile (for example, "Going to my 50th reunion, couldn't find my yearbook, thanks!!"). A 1940s-era pulp magazine with a lurid cover featuring a story titled "Juke Joint Girl" is now part of the collection of a juke-box museum in Copenhagen. An old children's storybook (*Goober Village*) made a special nostalgic gift for a buyer's grandmother. We still brag about our biggest sales: a signed book by Harry Houdini; a rare and collectible booklet about an exhibit on the sinking of the *Titanic*; and the report to the U.S. Senate on Fremont's expedition to Colorado and points west. Some unlikely items take on significance when the whole world is your marketplace.

We began online by listing items at low prices (our first sale was $3.25 for a back issue of an architectural magazine), but we now rarely list anything online at a price of less than $20. Our per-item average profit is now more than $25.00, after site fees and shipping.

CONCLUSION

The book sale truly "is the engine that powers our Friends group." It puts us in the public eye four times a year, and it brings in an amount of money that we'd be hard-pressed to achieve in any other way. It brings in new members too. People join to be able to come to the members-only presale on Friday night, and we take in at least twenty new memberships at every sale. Our online sales project has opened up some different ongoing volunteer opportunities and provided us with some great stories to tell.

Best of all, though, selling books gives eighty or so people (of our now 500-plus membership) a chance to volunteer and be an active part of the group. Some people enjoy doing a three-hour shift twice or three times a year, and others get acquainted at the sale and begin volunteering for other tasks. Because we take very seriously the term limits in our bylaws for officers and board members, we are always watching for possible new leaders to emerge, and many of our active leaders began as book sale volunteers. We've learned that the best way to keep volunteers coming back is to provide a friendly atmosphere and a meaningful and successful project to work together on. For us, selling used books has been the perfect combination of fundraiser and Friendraiser.

FOR MORE INFORMATION

Most of what we've learned has come from other Friends groups. Visit other book sales and take note of what they are doing. One way to find book sales in your area is to check www.booksalefinder.com.

United for Libraries is a division of the American Library Association created to serve library trustees, advocates, Friends, and foundations. Check out their web page (www.ala.org/united) for free resources. Consider joining their electronic discussion group—it's a great place to ask questions and learn what other Friends groups are doing.

4

Discovery Calls: Expanding Your Donor Base and Donor Pipeline for Future Library Support

Dwain Posey Teague

Academic Library Services (Joyner Library and the Music Library) and Laupus Health Sciences Library, East Carolina University

WHAT IS DISCOVERY WORK?

An ongoing challenge within the world of fundraising/development is increasing your library's donor base and establishing a pipeline of prospects/donors for future philanthropic support. While it is easy to go back to wonderful donors and ask them for additional support, it is crucial not to allow donors to burn out on any one organization. Continually expanding the donor base (donor pool) and establishing a pipeline of prospects/donors will ensure that there are enough donors to support an organization.

Within this chapter, several key fundraising-related terms and phrases are utilized. These include the following:

- Suspect—someone who has been identified as a potential prospect for the library, but little to nothing is known about them.
- Prospect—someone who has been identified as a potential donor for the library. Something is known about the person.
- Donor—someone who is currently supporting an organization.
- Discovery work/discovery calls—the process of engaging new prospects/constituents to determine their philanthropic interests as well as the possibility of their supporting one's particular organization. Equivalent to cold calling in sales.
- Donor cycle—the process of identifying a donor, engaging/cultivating a donor, soliciting a gift, closing a gift, and stewarding (thanking) a donor.
- Donor/prospect pipeline—the process of continually having prospects/donors moving through a cycle that ultimately will lead to philanthropic support.

- Donor base/donor pool/prospect pool—a group of donors/prospects for an organization.
- Gift capacity—based on public information, an estimated/on-paper idea of the size of gift a prospect/potential donor could possibly make to an organization if inclined to do so.
- Personal visit—meeting a prospect/donor in person to engage him or her and to discuss an organization and its needs. Personal visits may take place at an office, home, restaurant, and so on. Ultimately, within library development, having such a visit take place within the library is optimal so the visit can include a tour of the library.

Discovery work is a thrilling and yet challenging aspect of fundraising. Much like cold calling in sales, conducting discovery work requires a fundraiser to contact prospects who may have little or no contact with the organization, but based on research of public information, it is determined that the prospects may have the capacity to make significant/major gifts to an organization if so inclined. Conducting discovery calls may be intimidating to those who have not participated in the process—but don't let that stop you! Keep in mind that you are simply trying to raise funds and awareness for an important cause—your library. When reaching out to prospects or donors for the first time, it is not uncommon to have to attempt twenty to thirty contacts before securing an appointment. Engaging prospects or donors for future philanthropic support may require months or years of contact (cultivation) before a gift is made, but the time and effort are worth it when support for the library is received. You may be asking yourself, "Who are the people I'm supposed to be contacting for discovery contacts?" Possibilities include those listed below:

- Current donors: Review the donor database to identify donors who have been making continuous gifts to your library. Other than their name and address, do you know anything else about them?
- Volunteers: Current or past volunteers may be wonderful philanthropic donors, but maybe they have never been asked to give.
- Retired employees: Some retired employees may have had a wonderful career with your library. Visit them to see if you can learn more about them and their philanthropic interests.
- University/college libraries: Ask the central development office for research on alumni or friends of the university who may be librarians (current or retired); who serve (or previously served) on other library boards; who have given to other libraries; who work for companies that focus on

technology/informatics; or who are authors or who are involved in library-related fields (literacy, archives, library preservation/conservation, etc.).

TECHNIQUES FOR CONDUCTING DISCOVERY WORK

There are various techniques for conducting discovery work/discovery calls. Every fundraiser may approach this process differently, so there certainly is not a cookie-cutter approach to the process. Several techniques that you may utilize include the following:

- The true cold call—calling the prospect for introductions and to inquire about the possibility of setting up a personal visit. A fundraiser generally has some background information about the prospect, such as their degree, career, positions held, other organizations they support (based on published donor honor rolls), political contributions, LinkedIn information, and so forth.
- E-mail—e-mailing the prospect for introductions and to inquire about setting up a visit. The benefit of the e-mail contact is that links may be included to allow the prospect to quickly learn more about the organization and view the fundraiser's contact information. It also allows the prospect to respond when it is convenient for them.
- Snail mail—sending a hard-copy letter via U.S. mail. This process is generally utilized if no phone or e-mail information is available as a way of contacting the prospect. The benefit of the snail-mail approach is that hard-copy information/brochures/newsletters may be included for the prospect to review.
- Multiple approaches—in some instances, it is beneficial to send an e-mail/snail-mail note in advance of the cold call. This allows the fundraiser to give the prospect some notice/heads up so they can expect the call on a specific date and at a specific time.

THE TRUE COLD-CALL DISCOVERY CALL

When calling someone at their place of business, I prefer to call mid-morning or mid-afternoon during the week. If you encounter a "gatekeeper" or receptionist, know that his or her job is to screen incoming calls. Briefly introduce yourself and explain that Mrs. Jones is expecting your call regarding the ABC Library. If you are told that Mrs. Jones is not available, you can leave a brief message with your contact information and also ask if it's better to call back at another time. Be sure to make a note of the name of the person who is screening the call, as establishing rapport with that person can benefit you in the future.

If you are transferred in to Mrs. Jones, after briefly introducing yourself, ask if this is a convenient time to speak with her for just a few minutes. If she says no, ask when another time would be more convenient. If she says yes, proceed with a brief overview of why you are calling. As noted in the e-mail and snail-mail samples below, clarify that you are not calling to ask for a gift (it is not a solicitation call) but that you are conducting courtesy visits/calls on behalf of the library, and you would welcome the opportunity to meet her. If she responds positively, proceed with setting up the visit. If she replies with "No, I am not interested," it is perfectly acceptable to thank her for her time and ask if she may have other referrals to people who may be good contacts on behalf of the library. If I receive a "No" during a phone call, I generally will ask if they would like to be on our mailing list. It's also a good time to verify their other contact information.

When calling someone at home, as with a call to the office, I prefer to call mid- to late morning or mid- to late afternoon during the week. I avoid calling during lunch, in the evening, or on weekends. Respecting a constituent's personal time is important. No one likes being disturbed during dinner or when spending time with family and friends.

E-MAILS

When sending an e-mail to attempt a discovery call, ensuring the donor opens the e-mail is of utmost importance. Having a wonderfully written e-mail is moot if the recipient isn't inclined to open it. A well-written subject line is vital to this process. A generic subject line like "Hello from the ABC Library" or "Donor Visits for the ABC Library" is not as apt to be opened by the recipient. Personalizing the subject line as much as possible is beneficial. Examples include "Hello Mrs. Jones: Introduction from Dwain at the ABC Library"; "Hello Dan: Referral from Your Colleague Joe Smith"; and "Hi Susan: University Alumni Visits in Houston on November 13."

Next, the body of the e-mail is the second most important aspect of the discovery e-mail. Keeping the e-mail relatively brief and concise will ensure that the appropriate amount of information is conveyed but that it's not so much that the recipient is overwhelmed or confused. Personalizing the body of the e-mail if possible is also helpful; for example, thanking them for recent gifts or referencing the degree(s) the recipient received from the university. While many fundraisers may disagree, I sometimes note that the purpose of the visit is not to ask them for a gift (solicitation). My ultimate goal is to make a personal connection to learn more about the recipient to then identify what interests them philanthropically. Major-gift-level philanthropic giving is based on relationships. We fundraisers serve as liaisons between donors and the libraries for which we work. We strive to become familiar with what our donors are interested in and then attempt to present them with giving opportunities that will be of interest to them. Several sample e-mails are shown in the textboxes. Note that all example names and addresses are fictitious.

SAMPLE E-MAIL 1

Subject line: Hi Dr. Jones: ECU Medical School Alumni Visits in Jacksonville

Hello Dr. Jones:

Greetings from the Laupus Health Sciences Library at East Carolina University! My name is Dwain Teague, and I will be conducting courtesy visits with some of our School of Medicine and Nursing alumni throughout the Jacksonville area November 14, 15, and 19. If you and Mrs. Jones might have a few spare minutes that I could host you for coffee, lunch, or a visit at your office, it would be a pleasure to meet you both and to learn more about your experiences at ECU. Please rest assured that you will not be asked for a gift. ECU is trying to do a better job of reconnecting with our alumni around the country so we can hear about your experiences at ECU and how your time here impacted your career in the medical field.

Thank you so much for your time, and I hope schedules will allow an opportunity for us to meet briefly while I am in Florida in a few weeks. In the meantime, if I can be of any assistance to you on behalf of ECU and the School of Medicine, please don't hesitate to let me know.

Sincerely,

Dwain

P.S. You may enjoy perusing the ECU Brody School of Medicine site if you haven't been back to Greenville recently: www.ecu.edu/cs-dhs/med/index.cfm.

SAMPLE E-MAIL 2

Subject line: Hi Ms. Shrauger: ECU Friends of the Library Visits in New Bern

Hello Ms. Shrauger:

Greetings from the Joyner Library and the Music Library at ECU! My name is Dwain Teague, and I work with our Friends of the Library group. I am personally reaching out to current and former Friends of the Library members in the New Bern area to say hello and to ask if you may be receptive to a brief visit over coffee or lunch in the future. Our library dean, Jan Lewis, and I are working our way around the state personally visiting with our constituents to say hello and to update everyone on the wonderful things the ECU Libraries are doing for our students and faculty. As a librarian, you certainly know how important our work is and the impact it makes on our users.

If you are receptive to meeting us, we would welcome the opportunity to coordinate that visit when it's most convenient for you. Or, if you haven't been back to campus in a while, we would love to host you for a VIP tour and show you our Archives and Special Collections Area.

Thank you so much for your time, and if I can be of further assistance to you, please don't hesitate to let me know.

Sincerely,

Dwain

SNAIL MAIL

As noted above, sending a hard-copy letter can be utilized if no phone or e-mail information is available. The ability to enclose additional material (e.g., brochures or newsletters) is an advantage of this method of contact. Some sample letters are shown in the texboxes.

While the response all fundraisers want is "Yes, I would love to meet with you to hear more about the library!" many times the answer will be "No" or "Not now." It is important not to become discouraged by a response of "No." Unless the donor/constituent clearly expresses their wish to not hear from you or the organization again (in which case, document their wish as noted below), then a brief reply may yield a positive response in the future.

Thank you so much for your reply. I am sorry we will not be able to visit during my trip to South Carolina, but if you are receptive to a call in the future, I look forward to reaching out to you when I'm traveling in your area again. Until

---

SAMPLE HARD-COPY LETTER 1

December 6, 2014
Mr. Doug Price
432 Elizabeth Drive
Huntersville, NC 28078-3256

Dear Doug:

Greetings from East Carolina University! My name is Dwain Teague, and I will be conducting courtesy visits with many of our alumni and friends in the Charlotte/ Huntersville area January 14 and 15, 2014. The university is trying to do a better job of personally connecting with our alums to learn about your time as a student at ECU, to discover how your degree has benefited your career, and to hear your thoughts about ECU as it stands today. Please rest assured that you will not be asked for a gift. We want to hear your feedback and suggestions.

With your permission, I will call you after the holidays. We have your number as (704) 123-4567 on your alumni record. If your schedule allows 10 or 15 minutes that I could treat you to coffee, it would be a pleasure to meet you. Also, we are hosting an alumni event at the NASCAR Hall of Fame in Uptown Charlotte the evening of Tuesday, January 14, and another event the night of Wednesday, January 15 (location TBA, if you and your guests should wish to attend one of these events and meet other ECU alumni/friends).

Happy holidays!

Sincerely,

Dwain Posey Teague
Director of Major Gifts

---

then, if I can be of any assistance on behalf of the library, please don't hesitate to let me know. Should your travels bring you this way, we would welcome the opportunity to host you for a VIP tour of the library.

Another positive aspect of receiving an otherwise negative reply is that many e-mail replies will contain valuable contact information in the signature line. You may be able to update your contact information for someone based on their reply, including cell number, links to their website, additional mailing addresses, professional titles, and so on. As mentioned above, if someone responds that they absolutely do not wish to hear from your organization again or that they wish to be removed from your calling/mailing lists, then it's important to ensure that their request is respected and documented internally. Be sure to update your databases or spreadsheets to code constituents as "Do not call," "Do not mail/e-mail," "Do not contact," and so forth.

SAMPLE HARD-COPY LETTER 2*

Dr. Jeffrey Charles
321 Laurie Wooten Lane
Greenville, NC 27834-7613

Dear Dr. Charles:

Greetings from the Laupus Health Sciences Library at East Carolina University. As you may have read recently, Dr. Spencer retired as director of the Laupus Library in September. We are honored to have former ECU chancellor Richard Eakin serving as our interim director.

Dr. Eakin and I, along with Ms. Fiona Brock, one of our new librarians, would like to invite you for coffee or lunch at the Laupus Library so we can introduce ourselves and provide you with updates on behalf of the library. We also wish to personally thank you for your past generous support of the library. The exhibit gallery that you named continues to be one of the most popular areas within the library!

Should you wish to contact me, please feel free: teagued@ecu.edu or 744-0248. I heard wonderful things about you from Dr. Spencer, and we look forward to coordinating your visit when your schedule allows.

Thank you so much for your time and support.

Sincerely,

Dwain Teague
Major Gift Officer

*Hard-copy letter sent to donor who made a major gift before the arrival of the fundraiser and the current library dean (neither of whom had ever met the donor). The goal was to coordinate a personal visit with him in hopes of engaging for additional support.

SAMPLE HARD-COPY LETTER 3*

October 4, 2013

Ms. Joann Ridenhour
12345 69th Ave. NE
Saint Petersburg, FL 33704-4608

Hello Ms. Ridenhour:

Greetings on behalf of the Laupus Health Sciences Library at East Carolina University in Greenville, North Carolina. My name is Dwain Teague, and I serve as director of major gifts for the Laupus Library.

I am personally reaching out to our donors and friends in Florida to let you know that I will be in Florida conducting courtesy visits with our constituents to say hello on behalf of the Laupus Library and East Carolina University as a whole. The dates I am planning to be in Florida are tentatively November 13–20.

If your busy schedule may allow a brief opportunity for me to introduce myself and to personally thank you for your past support of the Laupus Fund here at the library, it would be an honor to meet you. I had the honor of personally knowing Dr. and Mrs. Laupus via my work with the ECU libraries years ago. They were truly wonderful people, and they left a lasting legacy here at the Medical Campus. We have a beautiful area on our fourth floor of the Laupus Library that is named in honor of Mrs. Laupus. It's known as the Evelyn Fike Laupus Exhibition Gallery. I've included a wonderful photo of the portrait of Mrs. Laupus and a photo of the gallery space.

Thank you so much for your time, and once again, if your schedule allows an opportunity for a brief visit over coffee or lunch, it would be a pleasure to meet you. Please rest assured that the purpose of this visit is not to solicit you for another gift, but to simply thank you and to provide you with updates as to how the Laupus Library is benefiting our medical and health sciences students and faculty.

Sincerely,

Dwain Posey Teague
Director of Major Gifts

*Hard-copy letter sent to donor who made a major gift before the arrival of the fundraiser and the current library dean (neither of whom had ever met the donor). The goal was to coordinate a personal visit while traveling to their state.

MULTI-APPROACH

Depending on how well you know the prospect/donor, contacting them initially via e-mail/snail mail may result in a more positive response when the call is made. This initial contact can give the donor advanced notice that you will be contacting them. If an e-mail or letter has been sent saying you will call them on a certain day at a specific time, it is imperative that you make a note on your schedule to make the call as planned and on time.

SAMPLE MULTI-APPROACH CONTACT

You may wish to utilize the previous e-mail/snail mail examples and include this statement: "With your permission, I will call your office on Monday, December 2, at 2:00 p.m. to introduce myself. I look forward to speaking with you then. Should you wish to contact me before then, please feel free: teagued@ecu.edu or (252) 123-4567."

Utilizing board members/volunteers/other donors to assist with introductions during the discovery process can be most beneficial. Having volunteers/constituents review lists of potential donors may result in names being identified that volunteers may know. In this case, utilizing the volunteer to assist with an introduction can be most beneficial so the fundraiser then can make a "warm call" on the prospect.

SELECT BEST PRACTICES FOR DISCOVERY WORK

In addition to the tips and suggestions offered above, you should have plans of action for conducting your discovery visits. What may interest one person will not necessarily interest another. Being able to offer an array of ways to meet with, and engage, a constituent will result in more positive responses and results.

Engaging Discovery Prospects Visiting Your Institution

Tours, after-work gatherings, lunch meetings, and so on are wonderful ways to engage discovery suspects/prospects. What better way to promote your library than to personally show it to suspects/prospects? Utilize your library, collections, and unique spaces/exhibits to engage new prospects. Invite prospects to VIP tours of your library and utilize colleagues (dean/director, associate directors, librarians, and staff members) to assist with the tours. It is impossible for me, the fundraiser, to know every aspect of the library.

I eagerly call on my colleagues who are experts within their fields to share information with visitors. Coordination and planning in advance are a crucial part of this process. Personally meet with colleagues in advance of the guest's visit to discuss the game plan for the visit to ensure everyone is on the same page. The fundraiser should provide everyone involved with brief talking points as to how the visit should proceed.

Simple ways to engage discovery suspects/prospects for their personal visit to the library include those listed below:

- Coffee/lunch with a director/dean/other library official. Many constituents will feel honored to have the opportunity to personally meet a director or another official at the library.
- "Behind the scenes" tours of the library: special collections/archives (if policies allow nonstaff to be escorted for tours); preservation/conservation labs; Interlibrary Loan; cataloging areas; and so forth.
- Utilization of special collections or subject-specific libraries to engage constituents who have a specific interest in that subject area; for example, if the constituent has a passion for music, collaborate with the head of the Music Library/Collection to provide a VIP tour of the Music Library/Collection.

The final textbox shows an example of using text within a card inviting prospects to a VIP visit at the library (the cover of the card is a beautiful image of the library). Space is provided for personalizing the card.

Dr. Richard R. Eakin, associate vice chancellor and Laupus Health Sciences Library director (interim), welcomes you for a personal visit at the Laupus Library. Depending on your schedule, you can enjoy a cup of coffee or a bite of lunch while hearing how the Laupus Library is assisting ECU's medical and health sciences students, faculty, staff, and members of the medical community throughout Pitt County and the region.

Please feel free to contact Dwain Teague at teagued@ecu.edu or 252-744-0248 to learn more or to discuss dates for your visit. Parking passes are provided to ensure that you can park close to the library entrance. Rest assured that you will not be asked for a gift. We are striving to ensure our friends and constituents stay abreast of the vital role the Laupus Library plays in the lives of the medical community at ECU and throughout the region.

Miscellaneous logistical details will ensure discovery visitors have a wonderful experience:

- Provide parking adjacent to the library (if possible), or assist as much as possible with parking.

- Explain who will greet them or what they should do upon parking.
- Send detailed maps/directions for parking, of the library, and so on. Include phone numbers and other contact information should the visitors become lost or run late.
- Greet the visitor to welcome them to the library. I personally like to greet my guests as they are parking so I can personally escort them into the library.
- Determine in advance whether the visitors have any food or beverage preferences or allergies if you are having a meeting that will involve food or beverages.
- Stay on schedule. If your visitors have a tight schedule, or you promised them their tour/visit would only last a specific amount of time, ensure that everyone stays on target to ensure the tour concludes at the appointed time.
- Share packets of information or other items for the visitors to take with them as the tour concludes. This will keep visitors from having to carry materials around during their tour.
- Send appropriate follow-up thank-you notes, and if the visitor asked for more information, ensure that the requested information is sent in a timely manner.

Meeting with Prospects Outside the Library

Plenty of opportunities exist for engaging discovery suspects/prospects who are not able to personally visit the library (they may have physical limitations that prevent them from visiting the library or they may live/work a great distance from the library). Take the library to them!

- Coordinate a special visit at someone's home or office.
- If there are unique items that are allowed to leave the library, utilize the appropriate library colleagues and take items for constituents to view. A librarian or other staff member can share great details regarding the items and the role they play within the collections. They also can speak personally about the need for financial support to benefit the library/collections. Some items that are always well received are photos from the archives that need identifying, yearbooks, and traveling exhibits.
- When traveling, host "lunch and learn" opportunities. Invite discovery suspects/prospects to enjoy a bite of lunch while watching/listening to a presentation regarding the library. Lunch gatherings work well for those who are on tight schedules, and they enable guests to network with each other.
- Host after-work gatherings that will enable discovery suspects/prospects to stop by after work to meet the fundraiser and library representatives.

Such after-work gatherings can be hosted at restaurants where guests can enjoy a beverage and an appetizer while learning more about the library and meeting other constituents. These events work well because they can be "floating," meaning guests can come and go as their schedules allow (I generally host these events from 5:30 p.m. to 7:00 p.m.). There will probably be other guests present, and many discovery suspects/prospects may feel more comfortable in a group setting vs. one on one.

Coordinating with Library Staff

The library fundraiser should work closely with library colleagues to know of their travel schedules for attending library conferences. If a librarian is attending the ALA Conference in Orlando, the fundraiser can plan personal discovery visits or group events in that area that will enable the librarian to attend and to represent the library. Coordinating schedules like this makes good use of travel budgets to combine conference and donor travel into one. Some discovery visits, however, may require travel simply to see specific people. If a suspect/prospect is identified and they live a great distance from the library, it may be worth the money to coordinate a special visit to go personally meet them. It is not necessary for the fundraiser to always have a library colleague participate in a discovery visit if schedules do not allow for multiple staff to travel.

Setting Goals

Setting goals for discovery work makes the process manageable. Goals may include the following:

- Attempting a specific number of discovery contacts within a time frame (e.g., twenty contacts per month).
- Attempting to personally engage every donor to your library within one year.
- Utilizing board members/volunteers to assist with at least one discovery-contact introduction per month.
- Planning in advance for work-related travel that will enable you to reach out to donors/prospects who do not live/work within close proximity to your library (e.g., if the ALA is meeting in Las Vegas, plan far enough in advance to identify donors/prospects in that area).

I generally block off parts of my schedule every few days to focus on making discovery calls or to focus on discovery work. Anyone who has ever conducted cold calls knows that it can be a somewhat draining process. Anticipating a positive response, receiving negative feedback, and attempting to make your pitch within a few seconds so you aren't on the receiving end of a hangup can be tedious. Breaking discovery work into small, manageable chunks is best. If I am making discovery calls for a specific time frame (such as in advance of a trip), I really must focus, as time is of the essence and I want to secure as many appointments/visits as possible.

CONCLUSION

The discovery-call process can be time consuming and challenging, but it certainly will result in new contacts and donors for the library. Every library, regardless of whether they are public, private, or academic, and re-gardless of whether they have a fundraiser/development officer, can utilize the discovery process. The library dean/director, or other library staff who are involved in outreach, can utilize the tips and suggestions within this chapter to further expand their prospect pool and donor pipeline, thus ensur-ing future philanthropic support. Going into discovery work knowing that rejection is a very real part of the process will make it much less daunting. Never take the rejection personally. As noted above, simply document the person's rejection, and if they provide you with the opportunity to reach out to them again, do so. As mentioned earlier, twenty to thirty true cold-call discovery attempts must be made before a visit is confirmed. Perseverance is crucial. Knowing that you are making discovery calls as a way to ensure your library will have the philanthropic support necessary to provide out-standing service is wonderful motivation!

5

The Campaign for Seattle's Public Libraries: Buildings, Programs, and Endowment

TERRY R. COLLINGS
Seattle Public Library Foundation

THE PATH TO SUCCESS

It was a brick-by-brick, step-by-step process that—in the end—paid off handsomely. By the close of the Seattle Public Library Foundation's Campaign for Seattle's Public Libraries in 2005, more than 22,000 donors (individuals, foundations, and corporations) had contributed over $83 million for new and expanded libraries across the city, expanded children's programming (plus endowment), expanded humanities programming (plus endowment), and greatly expanded collections of books and media (plus endowment).

Astute but skeptical readers may quickly conclude, "Yes, but that's Seattle, and we're not Seattle." In one respect, their observation would be dead on. Our results would not have been nearly this dramatic absent the great wealth and many philanthropists created by Microsoft's huge success. Yes, the number of thousands appearing on the bottom line of any major fundraising campaign depends in great degree upon the size, wealth, and civic commitment of a community's citizens. In Seattle, on all counts we happened to be more fortunate than most.

In another respect, however—and this point stands center stage for any organization in the fundraising business—the key elements of Seattle's success are little different from those of successful fundraising campaigns in communities of all sizes and shapes across America. The implementation details vary greatly, but to one degree or another, most share the following elements:

1. Strong, competent leadership at the top and in key staff/volunteer positions
2. A compelling vision, cause, or project

3. A solid support infrastructure
4. A donor-first focus (it's all about relationships)
5. Asking for financial support
6. Patience and persistence

If you read no further, reflect on how your library stacks up on these six elements. The remainder of this chapter explores how we addressed them because few were in place when I was hired as the library's first development professional in 1989, eight years prior to the launching of our capital campaign. Not only were few in place, but we also learned these lessons as we went along. Nothing beats getting into the trenches to learn what works, what doesn't work, and where to focus one's efforts. It took time, patience, and persistence.

IN THE BEGINNING

I was hired by a visionary city librarian, Liz Stroup, who had a large list of special programs and projects requiring support outside the library's limited operating budget for their implementation. At the same time, the library board of trustees realized that the members of the library's (then) foundation lacked familiarity and influence with Seattle's philanthropic leaders. While serving as strong personal advocates for the library, the foundation's members were not all that well connected nor were they comfortable asking for financial support.

The library board of trustees made the critical decision that my position was to be as a library employee providing staff leadership to the foundation board as it undertook fundraising efforts, but reporting to the city librarian as opposed to becoming a foundation employee. The latter option was somewhat of a moot point in our case, since the foundation didn't have the resources with which to hire a professional development officer anyway.

This reporting structure is not common among urban library systems in this country. In most systems, fundraising staff are employees of their library's foundation. Comparing the pros and cons of these two fundamentally different approaches likely would require a separate chapter in its own right. Suffice it to say that both models can—and do—work well *if* the chief development officer (whatever his or her title) and the library director work closely together in furtherance of the stated goals of the library itself. A library's foundation is—or should be—a partner of critical importance for furthering these goals.

In my many chance encounters over eighteen years at the Seattle Public Library and its foundation, it was rare to hear a donor say, "I give to the foundation." With evident pride they typically proclaim, "I give to the library" or "I support the library" or "I support what the library is doing with respect to [fill in the blank]." The donor's intent is that which must be honored regardless of the structure selected for acquiring and managing their gifts.

Successfully managing these structural relationships always comes down to mutual trust. Ours worked from the beginning because the city librarian knew that I was working closely with her to secure financial support for the library's priorities. This relationship with the foundation worked because (1) they understood and embraced their role from the moment they were incorporated in 1980, and (2) the city librarian and I respected, valued, and supported their many efforts. They took on the proposed projects they felt to be of importance to the people served by the library. We made a conscientious effort to report on foundation-supported programs and projects at their monthly board meetings.

THE CRITICAL BUILDING BLOCK YEARS

As I sat down at my desk for the first time in June 1989, I knew that I didn't have (1) a supportive infrastructure or system in place, (2) an existing donor base of any size to build upon, and (3) a foundation board that, in the near term at least, would be of much help in raising larger gifts.

What I did have was (1) an individual, Paul Feavel, assigned to work with me who proved to have terrific database creation and management skills (e.g., recording, tracking, acknowledging, and reporting donations), and (2) a single, compelling library need: Ramona. Ramona was lying in state in front of the library with her hood open. She was the library's beloved bookmobile needing to be replaced.

To have the replacement of a bookmobile as our first challenge couldn't possibly have been more propitious. Every third person seems to have a fond bookmobile memory or story. That being said, I can't emphasize enough how important it was for me to have the support of someone like Paul, who could attend to so many of the infrastructure details while I focused on the bigger picture. Competent, hard-working back-office support people are the real unsung heroes in this business. They're essential.

There was one other major factor at play in my thinking at the time. I knew it was important to show some early success, in large part because a few members of the foundation board were skeptical of the need for a "hired gun" (as one of them referred to me), and many members of the library's professional staff were equally, if not more, skeptical.

This put Paul and me on a dual course. As happens with most start-ups, I focused on the low-hanging fruit: foundations and the occasional corporation. Local foundations in particular were highly responsive to the new bookmobile project. It was something appealing, tangible, and limited in scope. This early success didn't go unnoticed within the library. A number of bright, creative staff members began to envision possibilities for their programs not formerly considered. A pattern was established that expanded over the next eight years.

With our help, library managers developed numerous projects for which we secured funding. The details of those aren't important other than that they were for things like a first-time literacy/ESL program coordinator; packets promoting reading to newborns; an after-school program for latchkey children; homework help collections; sets of books for book clubs to check out; the summer reading program; and, of course, many more books for the general collections.

Running parallel to the effort to generate grants in support of these programs and projects was the need to create and grow a base of smaller donors. Developing the systems and procedures to accomplish this took a great deal of time and effort, which is where Paul's skills made the difference. Within four months of establishing the development office, we tested raising smaller gifts from individuals via telephone appeals. Since we were not permitted to use the database of library card holders for contact purposes, we relied upon volunteers to review donor listings from other nonprofit reports, copy down the names, and look up phone numbers in the phone directory. We chose the telefunding option over mail because during this same timeframe, direct-mail appeals for new donors on the part of other nonprofits were resulting in response rates in the 1 percent to 2 percent range. Plus, we had only names and phone numbers—no addresses.

Looking up names in a phone directory isn't a viable strategy in today's world, but the results are illustrative of the great potential that lies with a public grateful for the services they've received from the library over the years. With the promise of a new bookmobile as its focus, a one-week test run was conducted. Not counting those who said they would consider making a donation, it resulted in outright pledges from 25 percent of the households that were reached. One in every four people contacted via a cold call made a pledge that almost all of them honored. When the "will consider" gifts came through, we ended up raising more than we had recorded in outright pledges.

Despite understandable misgivings on the part of some foundation board members, telefunding was used as the strategy of choice to both acquire and renew smaller donations. During each subsequent year, longer acquisition appeals were conducted, reaching more prospective donors. Each time the results were the same: 25 percent of people reached (mostly supporters of Seattle's civic, arts, and cultural organizations) made pledges with gifts averaging between $35 and $40. We learned that securing first- and second-time gifts was more productive if the appeals were for more specific, tangible needs. Once a track record was established, phoners were successful in persuading many to designate their gifts for "where needed most." Patience and persistence paid off.

In tandem with securing grants in support of various programs and building an expanding database of small donors was the third effort that characterized these early years: recruiting well-connected people to the foundation board. This task took much longer than expected (no surprise, I'm sure, to anyone who's been charged with that task). Probably the greatest challenge was the "critical mass" issue.

Since boards tend to attract new board members who largely reflect the interests and lifestyles of existing members, they often become self-perpetuating. I would find myself cringing whenever someone would suggest a new board member simply because he or she "loves books." Well, yes, most of us do. But the stated mission of the Seattle Public Library Foundation (to paraphrase) is to secure financial support for library programs and facilities above and beyond what the city's tax-based funding makes possible.

It is difficult to attract individuals with greater community familiarity and influence unless they see at least a few recognizable names on the board roster. Since like attracts like, a board needs a certain critical mass of the kinds of individuals it seeks in order to be successful in attracting the individuals it seeks—a Catch-22 (the irony of using a book-title metaphor to describe a need that gets beyond books).

In addition, the "movers and shakers" in a community typically are attracted to challenges that, in their own way, are larger than life and highly visible; the more compelling the need or vision, the better. In these early years, we had raised funds for many very worthwhile projects, but none were of the kind that grab and hold the attention of key influencers. We knew, however, that a major capital campaign for new and expanded libraries lay on the horizon.

In our case, the turnaround began with a single foundation board member, Bill Golding, who walked in some of these circles. When Bill became president in 1994, he made it his single goal to recruit more influencers. During his one year as president and then for the next two years as chair of the board's nominating committee, Bill attracted the small handful of people needed to wage any kind of major fundraising campaign. Over time they, in turn, attracted others. At times, it does come down to a single determined individual who really "gets it."

THE PIECES FALL INTO PLACE

By 1998 under the strong leadership of the new city librarian, Deborah Jacobs, the library had concluded a years-long planning effort to determine its system-wide capital needs (mostly buildings, furniture, and technology) for the coming years. Seattle's city council approved placing a $196.4 million bond measure before the voters in November of that year, and the library foundation board pledged to raise (1) $25 million for the remaining capital construction costs and (2) $15 million for enhanced collections regardless of the outcome of the election. The foundation also provided $200,000 toward the marketing campaign costs to promote Proposition 1: *Libraries for All*. Confident of a positive outcome, a grant request was submitted in advance to the William H. Gates Foundation (precursor to the Bill and Melinda Gates Foundation) for a lead gift to the anticipated capital campaign.

On November 3, 1998, the voters approved the $196.4 million bond measure by close to 70 percent. The next day, the library foundation was informed that the Gates foundation would provide a $20 million lead gift. The foundation board could have concluded that they were already halfway toward their goal and left it at that. They did not. There were many unaddressed needs remaining, so they raised their campaign goal to $60 million, thus committing themselves to raising $40 million *in addition to* the Gates foundation lead gift.

The expanded goal included the original $25 million for new and expanded libraries systemwide, $10 million for new technology, $17 million for enhanced collections, and $8 million in support of programming for youth, adults, and people with special needs. This mix of needs proved to be absolutely critical to the success of the campaign as it progressed. *Many six- and seven-figure gifts would not have been secured if the campaign had been for capital construction only.*

The question invariably asked is "How did you do it?" This is a direct question but not one as direct or easy to answer as most would hope. A number of factors played key roles. First and foremost, we had strong leadership in place on both the library end and the foundation end. Strong leaders make things happen. They deviate greatly in how they accomplish things, but they accomplish things nonetheless. With them in place, a major fundraising effort is more or less assured. Absent these elements, lesser results are equally assured.

Second, we now had a really compelling vision of what a great library system would look like. The booklet that the library prepared for Proposition 1 voters illustrated the benefits that would accrue to every neighborhood, Seattle being a city of proud, distinct neighborhoods. It was, in the first instance, a vision with a voters-first focus that easily translated into a donors-first focus as the private-sector campaign took shape. Three words, *Libraries for All*, said it all and said it better than the tomes over which expensive consultants might have labored.

Finally, we had put into place (1) a highly competent and dedicated development office staff to support a multifaceted campaign, (2) the necessary donor tracking/financial reporting systems so as not to get overwhelmed when the tsunami of contributions came crashing in, and (3) a foundation board up to the challenge. All were part of the infrastructure necessary for maximizing success.

Once the campaign was launched, our biggest challenge was to focus like a laser beam on what are called the lead gifts: the handful of gifts that will make the difference between total success and something less than that. Those few gifts typically account for 80 percent to 95 percent (sometimes more) of the total raised by the end of a major campaign. We knew them to be essential, but they presented us with somewhat of a conundrum at this point. Just when everyone was most charged up to start hosting house parties and other labor-intensive strategies was the time when we needed to be focusing on securing these lead gifts. It was essential not to be going off in too many directions at once, which required a sense of discipline on the part of both staff and campaign volunteers. For the handful of volunteers who had the most influence with the deepest pockets, this was their moment.

The year before our campaign's launch, I attended a two-and-one-half-day workshop on managing capital campaigns. The words of one of the instructors stuck with me long after I'd forgotten the many other pearls of wisdom offered during those sessions. This particular presenter opined that if you went into a major fundraising campaign with four or five really well-connected volunteers, you would be in great shape.

Truer words were never spoken. Our capital campaign director, Gilbert Anderson, along with five or six other members of the foundation board, was the driving force behind securing lead gifts of $500,000 and more (some, much more). Gil in his role as the campaign chair was far and away the most critical. Gil, a retired CEO, was a past president of the Seattle Public Library Foundation Board of Directors. Immediately following the voters' approval of the bond referendum, the mayor appointed him to the Seattle Public Library's five-member board of trustees. Gil didn't shy away from asking for financial support and wouldn't take "No" for an answer. He did all of this with exceptional poise, grace, and good humor.

City librarian Deborah Jacobs also played a central role via her active participation in much of the lead-donor cultivation and many of the actual solicitations. She was able—as volunteers frequently are not—to articulate the totality of the vision and provide prospective donors with detailed answers to their many questions. Everyone knew that this project was in good hands. The development office provided leadership and support to both the city librarian and the campaign volunteers and secured a healthy number of major gifts through their own efforts.

We began with a compelling vision of remaking the Seattle Public Library for the twenty-first century. The fulfillment of this vision consisted of seven components, each of which had its own fundraising goal, and some of which were increased over the course of the campaign as benchmarks were met or surpassed.

1. A magnificent new Central Library to replace the old one
2. Twenty-six new (including replacements), enlarged, or renovated branch libraries
3. Greatly enhanced collections—both current and future (via endowment)
4. Increased children's programming—both current and future (via endowment)
5. Increased humanities programming—both current and future (via endowment)
6. Programs for people with special needs—both current and future (via endowment)
7. Campaign unrestricted to use where needed most to ensure that all goals are met

THE EXECUTION

In general, this is how it played out. Staff worked with campaign leadership and volunteers to (1) identify prospective donors; (2) research and discuss each prospect's other associations, philanthropic interests, and participation levels; and (3) match them with the goal (or goals) that we felt would be of greatest appeal (i.e., donor-first focus). Based upon a prospect's giving history in similar major campaigns, we would attempt to identify a targeted ask-amount that would be a stretch but not totally off-putting.

I mentioned earlier that leaders make things happen. They accomplish things in accordance with their own styles but accomplish them nonetheless.

This was certainly the case with the half-dozen Seattle Public Library Foundation members who went forth to raise a good many of our largest gifts. There were no "templates" as to how to proceed, but there were some general characteristics they shared in common.

All were socially active, tending to walk in various circles outside of their closest friends and associates. They frequently served with well-connected people on other charitable boards. This translated into their feeling more comfortable approaching varying sources with varying interests. Each was successful within his or her own broad sphere of influence.

You would be justified in thinking that it must be more complex than this. Well, no, it actually isn't. The simple truth is the right people at the helm tend to create their own momentum. That single piece of advice from the two-and-one-half-day workshop I took was worth many times the price of admission.

Our campaign leaders did expect good back-up support to provide them with whatever they felt they needed to call on a prospective donor. That varied from person to person, which is where the need for flexibility becomes especially important. In general, most volunteers wanted only a two-page letter or document summarizing the particular aspect(s) of the broader campaign that their prospect was being asked to support.

This is where our experience differs from the advice of many campaign consultants who insist you need to have a comprehensive, classy-looking document making your case for support. We actually spent a great deal of money for the design and production of a beautiful, well-produced booklet, but I don't think it made a difference in a single gift of any size.

This may not be true for other kinds of institutions whose missions may not be as well-known or widely admired. There's no question that we benefited greatly from the breadth and depth of the community's genuine love, respect, and trust for the Seattle Public Library. This may be part of the reason why our volunteers felt they needed only the briefest of summaries to make their calls on prospective supporters. In a very real sense, the "case for support" had been in the making for a long, long time. The same is true for most public library systems.

Generating support for endowments tends to be more of a challenge for more cerebral areas like the humanities—as opposed to scholarships, for instance, which are more tangible. For us, humanities programming translated mostly into literary and historical programs for adults. Within two months of the launch of our capital campaign, we decided to apply for a $500,000 National Endowment for the Humanities (NEH) three-for-one matching challenge grant. If approved, it would require us to raise $1.5 million to earn NEH's $500,000 match for a total $2 million endowment.

To secure approval, however, we learned it was highly advisable to have already received some advance commitments toward our $1.5 million portion. For that reason, we asked some of our current and former foundation members to consider designating their campaign pledges for this purpose. Enough members did so that the NEH application was submitted with $450,000 in pre-commitments. Application approved.

Entering the home stretch of the NEH subcampaign, our last $500,000 hurdle illustrates the value of having a mix of goals and being both flexible and creative as the campaign progresses. A donor self-identified who was interested in supporting, in her father's memory, an annual public lecture on American history by notable historians. We agreed that such a program would have great appeal to our library users and calculated that it would take a $500,000 endowment to support such a venture year after year. NEH challenge completed.

A number of other interested individuals self-identified along the way as well. One was the then director of the Starbucks Foundation. He arranged for us to hold a foundation board meeting at the Starbucks headquarters. Founder and CEO Howard Schultz made a short appearance and told us a story. Growing up poor in Brooklyn, he had vivid recollections of waiting for the bookmobile with his mother and being issued his first library card. The bookmobile and the books it brought had a profound effect on his upbringing. It helped him understand that there was a much bigger world outside the projects.

He noted that while there are lots of people making money, many more are being left behind. His goal was to provide the underserved with ongoing access to the same resources available to the very wealthy. We now knew how to focus our appeal. Not surprisingly, the grants from both the Starbucks Foundation and Schultz's own family foundation were for the endowment serving people with special needs. While few communities have a Howard Schultz per se, most do have people who have done well financially, some of whom have library stories to tell.

It was vital to uncover those stories because they informed us about people's underlying passions. Ferreting out these stories requires reducing the six degrees of separation to one or two degrees of separation. It still comes down to who knows who can open the right doors. Over the course of the campaign, it wasn't just the half-dozen volunteers who made this happen. Many other members of the foundation board assisted as well in making connections that resulted in large—if not lead—gifts of varying amounts. It was a *team effort* throughout.

As the campaign progressed, we experienced motivating forces not necessarily anticipated at the beginning. One was the appeal that the architect selected to design the new Central Library would have on certain individuals. When Rem Koolhaas's design was unveiled in 2001, it was indeed looked upon as a real "cool house" in the eyes of many. Once construction was well under way, we began hard-hat tours of the emerging library. Several individuals participating in those tours became six- and seven-figure donors. Some were people new to philanthropy and not on everybody's radar screen. Actually seeing the vision take shape captured their imagination and interest. The tours continued throughout the construction period and resulted in gifts at the $10,000–$25,000 (and under) levels as well.

For the capital construction portion of the overall campaign, it proved highly beneficial to focus our appeals on the two umbrella needs: (1) the Central Library, and (2) the branch libraries collectively, without attempting to set campaign goals for each individual branch library. First of all, with twenty-six different branch projects of varying degrees of complexity, individual fundraising goals would have been an administrative and accounting nightmare of epic proportions.

Treating the branch library campaign as a unit provided the library's capital construction team with maximum flexibility to use the funds where they were most needed. While some people chose to designate their gifts for particular branch libraries, these proved to be a very small portion of the total capital gifts raised and were easily accommodated.

Naming opportunities were, of course, highly important to some donors. Naming opportunities in both the Central Library (see Figure 5.1) and the branch libraries were kept to a minimum to avoid the impression that the libraries were built primarily with private support. They were not. Seattle's taxpayers assumed 85 percent of the overall capital construction costs. The library foundation declined the temptation to affix names on every table, chair, computer, and bookshelf in these libraries.

The bar for a naming right was set fairly high, especially in the Central Library, where it began at $250,000. Naming opportunities in the branch libraries were generally limited to four per branch (e.g., reading area, children's area, meeting room) and were generally in the $50,000–$100,000 range. A naming opportunity was in no way associated with the use of the donor's gift (a second administrative nightmare averted). A person could designate the use of a $100,000 gift for one of the program goals, for example, and be recognized in a neighborhood library meeting room pegged as a $100,000 naming opportunity. This strategy was also designed to provide maximum flexibility in the use of gifts.

At the same time, it was a library board of trustees policy that all new and rebuilt branch libraries were to be named *only* for the neighborhoods they served (e.g., Ballard, Beacon Hill, Montlake; see Figure 5.2). Once again,

Figure 5.1.   New Central Library. (Credit: Photo courtesy of the Seattle Public Library)

Figure 5.2.   New Beacon Hill Branch. (Credit: Photo courtesy of the Seattle Public Library)

public libraries are owned by the citizens. The new Central Library was to be named just that, even though there were a couple of efforts afoot to have it named in honor of leading civic leaders who had recently passed away.

Some donors declined the offer of having spaces named in their honor. In one instance I lost sight of my donor-first rule and almost paid for it "in perpetuity." One of Seattle's most remarkable and beloved philanthropists, whom I will call "Betty," had contributed several million dollars toward our children's programming endowment but did not want anything named for her. Sadly, as completion of the new Central Library neared, Betty's terminal cancer was taking a turn for the worse. An idea to have a landscaped area named in her honor after her death was being floated, but Betty caught wind of it and called. She informed me that if we proceeded as planned, she would haunt me for the rest of my days from wherever she was. Knowing Betty, she would have done it. Crisis averted.

The number of staff required to manage a capital campaign and the related costs to support the campaign are almost impossible to generalize since the answer to both depends to a great degree on whether a campaign goal can be fulfilled with relatively few large gifts, many smaller gifts, or a combination of the two. Our campaign was the last option. We generated some exceptional gifts, which kept the cost per dollar raised very minimal. This lead-gifts effort was complemented by a very aggressive grassroots campaign that resulted in many thousands of small gifts (for which the cost per dollar raised is much greater). Most campaigns are advised to increase their capital campaign goal by 10 percent to cover their fundraising costs. In other words, the projected costs should be built into the goal itself.

Due to the variety and complexity of fundraising strategies employed and the sheer volume of gifts to process, we had ten development office employees at any given time at the height of our campaign. We did not make extensive use of campaign counsel, which helped keep costs down.

MOVING FORWARD

At the campaign's end in 2005, a challenging task faced by most organizations coming off a major fundraising effort awaited us: how to convince the vast pool of new donors that their continuing support was crucial to the library's ongoing success. We conducted a donor survey to learn more about what motivated the foundation's largest campaign contributors and what they felt to be the best uses of additional private support in the coming years.

We sent a survey to approximately 200 donors who had contributed $10,000 or more to the Campaign for Seattle's Public Libraries. Fifty-seven percent responded. With seven options from which to choose, these donors overwhelmingly indicated that their primary motivation for giving to our library was that "the library is the one community resource that provides access to information for everyone." When asked to look forward in time and tell us what they considered the best uses of private funds down the road, the responses resulted in a tie between (1) expanding the library's collections of books and resources and (2) providing programs for children and teens.

This postcampaign feedback validated assumptions made going in. When all was said and done, it was of little surprise that 45 percent of the funds raised was designated for collections and program goals (especially their endowments), 43 percent was directed to the collective capital construction goals, and the remaining 12 percent was directed to where it was needed most.

Two final kudos are in order. One is to Microsoft cofounder, Paul G. Allen, whose foundation provided a second $20 million grant to the campaign. We wouldn't have exceeded $83 million without his family's very generous support. The second kudo—the one most relevant to other libraries—is that a foundation board that had never before raised more than $1 million in a single year *was determined to raise an additional $40 million on top of the two mega-grants from Microsoft's cofounders*. Under the leadership of Campaign Chairman Gil Anderson and City Librarian Deborah Jacobs, and with a development office staff coordinating the many moving parts, the foundation exceeded that goal. That determination represents the bookends to this campaign's success.

One major element is missing from this narrative. I have alluded to a large-scale grassroots fundraising effort that produced 99 percent of the 22,000 donors but have said little about it. We deemed this effort worthy of a chapter in its own right for two reasons. First, many readers may represent library constituencies for which broad-based fundraising is more realistic than major-gift fundraising. Second, the strategies used to secure these gifts are many and varied, thus deserving of their own narrative.

In 2001, I hired Jonna Ward as the director of the community campaign portion of our overall capital campaign. Her amazing efforts in that regard, combined with her continuing success in building the Seattle Public Library Foundation's base of supporters, are the subject of Chapter 6. She succeeded me as the foundation's executive director.

CONCLUSION

Suffice it to say that public libraries are the kinds of institutions that people like to support for all of the reasons described in this chapter. They know their tax dollars support the basic operations of their libraries but will make additional contributions if convinced their gifts will provide a margin of excellence in areas near and dear to their hearts. In this rapidly changing digital environment, the need for "bricks and mortar" may be receding as innovative service-delivery models become the bigger challenge.

That's an easy pivot for public library fundraisers. That which motivated so many donors to Seattle's campaign was not just inspiring architecture and larger spaces but also what our libraries *offered*: information access and resources coupled with programs and services for children, teens, and people with special needs. Patrons and donors alike still want the library's many constituents served consistently and served well. It is up to each and every one of us to keep pace with evolving methodologies and create visions that inspire. With strong leadership at the top and supportive infrastructures within, libraries can still think big.

6

Taking a Campaign Public: The Community Phase of the Campaign for Seattle's Public Libraries

Jonna Ward
Seattle Public Library Foundation

The first big fundraising campaign undertaken by an organization has the potential to transform its board, develop new staff expertise, and have a lasting impact for those who benefit from the organization's mission. It will change the culture and create new capacity that didn't exist before. That is what happened in Seattle beginning with the launch of what turned out to be an $83,000,000 campaign.

What follows is a continuation of Chapter 5 written by Terry Collings, retired executive director of the Seattle Public Library Foundation. He was the person who hired me for the community phase of the Seattle Public Library's major capital campaign. I came to the library foundation with a passion for libraries and a background in direct marketing. It was my experience as a direct marketer that drove the overall plan to implement and fulfill the goals of the community campaign.

This chapter focuses on the Seattle Public Library Foundation's community phase of its capital campaign (also known as the community campaign), the principles it was based on, and the tools used to complete the work. Reading Chapter 5 will put this information in context because the two campaigns are so interconnected; in Chapter 5, Terry Collings shows how the foundation secured major donations before turning its attention to the smaller donor. Roughly 75 percent of the campaign monies had been secured before the community phase was even launched to the public.

THE IMPORTANCE OF A
COMMUNITY PHASE IN A MAJOR CAMPAIGN

Whether you call it the public phase, grassroots effort, or community campaign, the idea is that any major campaign undertaken by a public library provides an extraordinary opportunity to develop a partnership with your community that ensures an enduring base of support long after the traditional capital campaign is completed. Usually donations generated during the community campaign are small gifts that come from many people. This is directly opposite to the phase of a campaign focused on major donors. A community campaign can increase visibility for your organization and in turn create "ownership" by the community and increase awareness of the library's need for private support. In the long run, this makes the job of the person responsible for securing "more support" in the future that much easier. And support isn't just about donations; it is about having an identifiable group of individuals who believe in the mission of the library, who will vote for your levies, and who will advocate for your system with elected officials. In a nutshell, the community phase of any major campaign is really about creating and securing your library's future.

Public libraries are uniquely positioned to leverage grassroots fundraising to generate small gifts and build a broad base of support. There are few other institutions that have such a wide array of people from which to draw. Many people in your community will have an affinity for libraries because chances are, at some time in their life, they have benefited or found enjoyment from a library. Your success comes with connecting to that goodwill. This is not an inexpensive or easy endeavor, but it is one that has long-term return on investment (ROI).

PREPARING FOR THE COMMUNITY PHASE

As in any successful fundraising operation, a key to your success rests with organizational readiness. Following are the steps—what we call the "four Ds"—for preparing for the community phase.

1. Discover—Doing a Comprehensive Review

Whether you plan to hire staff, contract with a vendor, or do this work yourself, this first step is about getting familiar with what you have to work with and where you are lacking. What institutional knowledge is there from any efforts in the past? What staff expertise and knowledge can you tap? Do you have a good repository for information in the form of a donor database? What donor lists might you have to start from?

2. Differentiate—Understanding Your Donors and Prospects

By the time your organization is ready to tackle the community phase of a campaign, you should have some kind of list of donors and people who care about your library. Other lists could exist, such as people who have attended planning meetings or members of your Friends of the Library. The more you know about your current supporters, the better luck you will have in finding more donors that look like them.

Not all donors are created equal, and it is fundamentally important to understand who your supporters are. Think of a donor base as a stock portfolio. There are many different kinds of people motivated by different things. By understanding the demographic and behavioral aspects of your donors, you can create segments of donors. Once you have formed segments, you can create key messages and emotional positions that will be compelling to them.

3. Develop—Having the Tools Needed to Create and Implement the Campaign

A campaign plan is a fundamental tool that acts as your "implementation roadmap." Your plan will include goals, strategies and tactics, a contact plan, and key messages. At the end of the chapter, you can see the plan we created to guide our work.

4. Decipher—Tracking, Learning, and Iterating

If you approach this work as a direct marketer would, you will commit to track what you do, measure the outcomes, analyze your results, and use what you learn to shape your next effort. This means at the early stages that you are testing ideas, learning what works best, and taking the winning messages, formats, and scripts and rolling out the winning concepts.

CASE STUDY OF THE SEATTLE PUBLIC LIBRARY FOUNDATION'S MY LIBRARY COMMUNITY CAMPAIGN

With the Seattle Public Library Foundation's major capital campaign launched in 1998 and well on its way to meeting its goal, the foundation leadership was looking for experienced professional staff to head up the community campaign. The community-phase fundraising goal was set at $2.5 million in small gifts to be matched by a $5 million challenge from the William H. Gates Foundation (later to become the Bill and Melinda Gates Foundation). Small gifts were defined as less than $10,000, and the match was $2 for $1. Their specific challenge was to encourage fundraising from the community, and we had three years in which to complete the challenge and earn the match.

In addition to generating new donors and gifts, the community campaign was designed with other goals in mind. It provided an opportunity to broaden visibility of the foundation and increase awareness, securing "ownership" from the community at large and thereby helping ensure a sustainable future of enhancement funding for the library. The overall strategy for the community campaign was to start with fundraising efforts—primarily telefunding and direct mail—that could be scaled up to generate the bulk of our small gifts. Then more broad-reaching awareness and grassroots efforts would be added to engage the community at large, connect with donors, and sustain long-term support.

The majority of the community campaign fundraising goal was completed between late 2001 and the opening of the Central Library in May 2004, when the matching challenge was fulfilled. However, since branches were still scheduled to open after 2004, the community campaign was able to continue to raise support even after the completion of the challenge match and has never really stopped generating support for the Seattle Public Library.

Preparing for the Public Phase of the Campaign

Community campaigns can be expensive, and Terry Collings, the foundation executive director at that time, did an excellent job of setting expectations with the foundation board. The board went into the community campaign understanding that it was our goal to break even on new donor acquisition that could cost up to $1 to raise $1. He also helped them understand that this form of fundraising would be drastically different from that of major gifts. Because our board had little experience with the public phase of a campaign, a Marketing Advisory Committee comprising board members and outside marketing experts was established. This gave comfort to the foundation board members.

Organizational Readiness

Organizational readiness was extremely important for the community campaign. This meant looking at our infrastructure from many different perspectives. We assessed staff to make sure we had the professional and support staff necessary to run a "fundraising machine." Two staff members with specialized skill and expertise were responsible for database management and gift processing support. Two experienced in-house telefunding professionals were responsible for calling existing small donors along with outside professional telefunding firms to focus on new donor acquisition. An advertising/direct-marketing firm was hired for creative development, and another small firm provided outsourced support for production resources.

The quality of our database was fundamental to our success. It was important to have a clean and efficient repository of information, a way to track our contacts and solicitations, donor behavior (gifts and attendance at foundation programs and events), and demographics (third-party or collected). Since we were aiming to generate a very high volume of gifts, we had to have the ability to process and acknowledge donors in a timely and manageable way.

Website Development

In 2002, donors were beginning to rely more on the Internet to research organizations, and they were looking for information about our campaign online. Donors had also begun to ask about making their gifts via the web.

The existing website had a limited number of static information pages. A task force of foundation and web-experienced library staff was formed. Their charge was to develop a plan for the strategy, design, content, implementation, and ongoing support of the foundation web presence. The foundation website was designed to

- tell our story and give authenticity and legitimacy to foundation fundraising activities;
- provide the opportunity to give online or to print a gift form; and
- recognize the campaign donors and volunteer board.

A "request for proposal" process was used to find a web design firm to complete this work using a partially paid/pro-bono arrangement. Within the first year after the site went live, we secured two $10,000 gifts that originated from people who had never supported us before and had used the website to research our efforts.

Identity and Communications

The messaging and communication needs for the community campaign were different from what was done for the silent phase/major donors. Since the connection of the small donor prospects was to the library (as most had no idea who or what the foundation was), we wanted to make sure we didn't confuse people by introducing the foundation as a new entity, with its own logo distinct from that of the library. Around this time, the library was working on overhauling its logo for a more modern look that could be used as the new branches were completed. This provided the opportunity to consider dropping the unique foundation logo and identity (see Figure 6.1). The rationale was that it would be very hard to establish/create recognition of a separate identity for the foundation and that this might actually hinder us in our fundraising. After much discussion, the foundation adopted a form of the newly designed library logo (see Figure 6.2). The library and foundation logos could stand alone or work in tandem to maintain a clean and simple brand.

The community campaign also needed to develop a strong and compelling way to talk about our campaign. We created a "messaging platform" that guided written content across many different media, ensuring a unified message and theme. A search was done to find an agency partner who could support the awareness and direct-marketing aspects of the campaign. A local firm was selected based on its compelling message platform. They brought in a partner to handle the public relations aspect of the work.

The overarching theme that was developed was the simple but powerful "My Library." It was based on interviews with library patrons, donors, and the public in general. When asked about the library, people kept saying, "At my library . . ." This simple and personal theme served as an effective

PLACES ALIVE WITH POSSIBILITY.
IMAGINE SEATTLE'S LIBRARIES

Figure 6.1. Former foundation logo, which was distinctly different from the library logo.

Figure 6.2. New foundation logo, which aligned with the library logo and color scheme.

umbrella that could be personalized to reflect a wide variety of audiences. Regardless of what creative was used, we were always trying to convey a single-net impression that would leave the recipient of our message thinking, "I love my library, and I will personally do everything I can to continue to improve it." This theme also allowed us to tailor our messages to the different segments/affinity groups in which we looked for donors. All office papers, newsletters, and giveaways were incorporated into the My Library theme for a unified and consistent platform.

Executing the Community Campaign

Once the infrastructure was in place throughout the preparation phase, the foundation embarked on a multifaceted campaign that included the fundraising effort, an awareness component, and a grassroots phase. The fundraising took place throughout the whole campaign. At the same time, we started our awareness work, followed by the grassroots phase (see Figure 6.3).

Fundraising Plan

We set out to create and implement a multichannel fundraising plan designed to acquire new donors as well as renew and up-sell our base of ap-

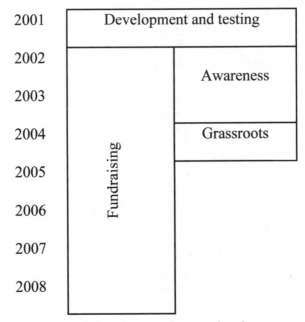

Figure 6.3.   Timing of community campaign phases.

proximately 5,000 households who had donated in past years. These donors had been generated utilizing telefunding through the campaign some years earlier plus an annual campaign to secure gifts from the contacts generated by the board members.

One challenge faced in the community campaign was that people didn't automatically think of the library for philanthropic gifts. But we had the advantage that the library services touched such a large cross section of the Seattle population. We also leveraged the challenge match from the Gates Foundation, offered flexibility on how the donor could designate their gift (where needed most, books and resources, or for library programs), and provided benefits for all giving levels—plus donors could have up to three years to pay off their pledges.

Knowing that telefunding had been successful in the past just by using names in the phone book, we put our initial focus on acquiring lists and testing messages via the phone. Databases of people with phone numbers are compiled by various vendors using many sources of data. After reviewing vendors and holding an initial trial, with the help of a list broker, we were able to negotiate a five-year agreement for unlimited use of a database, which was imported into our own system. While this was a lot of upfront work, it proved extremely valuable as it allowed us to track whom we solicited. It also supported the use of barcodes on our reply devices, which greatly increased efficiency in processing gifts from a record in the database rather than starting from scratch at the point of gift entry.

The phone campaign was initially set up to roll across the city, targeting zip codes that aligned with branch construction activity. After this first pass through the city, we focused on the areas in which we were most successful and had a reasonable return on investment for new donor acquisition.

Even with this database, we anticipated that we could not raise enough gifts through telefunding alone. Direct mail had not been effective in the past but was the best way to reach more people. If we could make the same database work for mailing as for phoning, it would save us an incredible amount of money compared to renting lists of known, direct-responsive subscribers and donors to other organizations. A key to our success came with the testing of segments of the compiled database.

Awareness Efforts

To facilitate our fundraising, we wanted to generate as much awareness as possible for the fundraising the foundation had undertaken. The fact that branch libraries were beginning to open certainly helped, but there was an opportunity to do more. Our awareness strategy was executed using a number of tactical efforts.

- In-branch displays were put in place including a campaign brochure with a gift form and later a stand-alone gift envelope.
- A poster series of three distinct My Library stories was created to attract the attention of various target audiences. This was distributed via branch libraries and throughout the city using a posting company.
- A public service announcement (PSA) was developed and ran on one of our major local TV affiliations and was funded by a corporate sponsor.
- A local radio station whose listeners were aligned to our target audience became a media sponsor and ran our PSA on the station.
- Our daily paper donated premium advertising space, which was the beginning of a long-term partnership that evolved into a very effective way to promote library programs.

A large corporation based in Seattle was approached to be the My Library Community Campaign Premier Sponsor. In addition to cash support to help

underwrite branch opening celebrations, they provided in-kind gifts of refreshments that allowed the library to offer free, high-quality beverages and
pastries for three years at the library's newly established public programs.
This sponsor was recognized on all community campaign materials.

Grassroots Involvement

Knowing that everyone in the city would not be able to donate to the
campaign, we did try to be inclusive through our I Love My Library Story
Contest. The contest launched three months before the opening of the new
Central Library. Entry forms were distributed in branches and online via the
foundation and library websites and through advertising space donated by
our newspaper partner. The online materials were translated into Spanish,
Korean, Chinese, Vietnamese, and Russian. Special efforts were made with
the help of staff to get the materials to schools, child-care centers, senior
centers, and ESL services.

The contest was promoted by our media partners, and a local cable company joined in as well. We received two weeks of on-air promotion from our
cable partner; a half-page print ad ran weekly over four weeks; and our campaign sponsor displayed posters and materials in their retail stores throughout
Seattle for two weeks.

At the end of the contest, there were 426 entries from all parts of the city
and some from the county. Several schools sent in entries that were obvi-
ously assigned as homework; many came from seniors; and entries in all
six languages were submitted. All the entries were organized and read by a
volunteer, who selected the top fifteen in each age category. (This proved to
be a meaningful way to engage and cultivate a volunteer who became a major
donor, who later was asked to join the foundation board, and who eventually
became the foundation president!) The top fifteen contest entries from each
category were then judged by a committee that included library staff, foundation board members, and Friends board members.

Three winners from each of five age groups were selected, and one extra
from the large pool of seniors—for a total of sixteen winners. The coveted
prize was to be first in the door at the grand opening of the new Central
Library. The winners were all greeted by the mayor and given a special gift
basket from our community campaign premier sponsor. The entries proved to
be a treasure trove of stories that we have leveraged in our appeals, materials,
and countless other ways.

Results of the Community Campaign

From the fall of 2001 through 2005, more than 22,000 donors supported the
Campaign for Seattle's Public Libraries, with the bulk of donors coming from

our community campaign efforts. The information following reflects gifts from both new and existing small donors (defined as gifts smaller than $10,000). Nearly 485,000 solicitations were attempted via telefunding and direct mail, resulting in over 48,000 gifts worth over $3,800,000 plus the $5,000,000 match for the neighborhood libraries. Telefunding was, by far, the key to our success in terms of funds raised. While many organizations and boards shy away from this, it was the mainstay of our community campaign.

Based on tracking and analysis, our profile of the most responsive small donor was that of a homeowner and empty-nester with an income of $50,000-plus (strongest band was $50K–$74K), and thirty-five-plus years of age (the strongest band was sixty-five to seventy-four). Men and women responded equally. We also learned that the records in the database with phone numbers and a full name (rather than initials for the first name) were the most responsive to our solicitations via telephone or direct mail.

Telefunding Results

Utilizing in-house telefunding staff and two outside service bureaus, we made more than 375,000 solicitations across the city, resulting in more than 43,000 gifts worth nearly $3.3 million (see Table 6.1).

Table 6.1.   Results of Telefunding

	Results
Number of attempted phone solicitations	375,000
Number of realized gifts	43,500
Amount of realized gifts	$3,295,000
Average amount per gift	$76

Direct-Mail Results

To maximize direct mail, we aggressively tested offers that included incentive gifts, creative executions (envelopes, brochures, and reply devices), and list segments to find the most cost-efficient and effective mailings. Over 100,000 pieces of mail were sent, generating a 4.5 percent response rate for both new donor acquisition and additional gift solicitations (see Table 6.2).

Table 6.2.   Results of Direct Mail

	Results
Number of direct mail solicitations	110,000
Number of realized gifts	4,500
Amount of realized gifts	$505,000
Average amount per gift	$112

Return on Investment

Beyond dollars raised, the return on investment was nearly equal between telefunding and direct mail. However, when possible, the phone was our preferred method because it allowed greater reach and the opportunity for a conversation with a member of the community who supported our non-fundraising objectives. Plus, it raised over six times as much money!

Long-Term Capacity Building from a Community Campaign

The true legacy of the My Library Community Campaign was the opportunity to build a passionate and engaged foundation donor base for the library. Many of the new donors who made small first gifts during the campaign have become highly valued annual donors and advocates. Given how difficult and costly it is to build a small donor base, the Seattle Public Library Foundation is committed to continuing its work with these donors for the long haul.

The concept of capacity building has played out many times over. Whether offering unrestricted annual gifts or supporting our advocacy work and making calls to our elected officials about their interest in protecting the library, our small donors represent a very important segment.

In 2005, following several years of budget cuts to the library's operating funds, the City of Seattle had a surprise $55 million budget surplus in revenue, but the mayor didn't include the library in his allocation proposal to the city council. Two council members who were avid library supporters cosponsored a proposal to use a portion of the surplus for the library. Three more votes were needed from the other council members.

We turned to our donors, using a combination of e-mail and phone calls to reach them. Over the weekend before the vote, our donors flooded the voice-mail and e-mail boxes of our elected officials. This effort was credited with securing an extra $2.46 million for the library! (For a sample of the e-mail message sent to donors, see the textbox on the following page.)

CLOSING THOUGHTS ON A COMMUNITY CAMPAIGN

There are so many benefits from the effort to build and steward a small donor base. Here are a couple more points to think about. The Seattle Public Library Foundation is one of the few library foundations not reliant on ticketed fundraising events, such as a galas, luncheons, or breakfasts. While many organizations make them work, they can be incredibly staff and volunteer intensive and may net less than an organization hopes. Plus, our small donors also seem very resilient to economic downturns.

E-MAIL SENT TO DONORS TO HELP SECURE
$2.46 MILLION IN ADDITIONAL FUNDING FOR THE LIBRARY

Subject: Are Great Libraries a Priority?

The answer, believe it or not, may be in your hands. The Seattle Public Library's support from the city for books and materials and for open hours has declined even as demand has increased with the many new and expanded libraries that have opened over the past several years. Library staff have taken four furloughs (leave without pay or benefits) in order to soften the blow to the public. Now it's the city's turn to weigh in.

Next year, the city is anticipating a $55 million budget surplus. How much of that $55 million has been earmarked for Seattle's libraries for 2006? Zero. *Not a dime.* Council members Peter Steinbrueck and Jean Godden want to change that. They are co-sponsoring *a proposal to allocate $2.8 million to the Seattle Public Library budget* as follows:

- $1 million to restore much of the reductions in the library's collections, including books, magazines, DVDs, and other resources
- $1.8 million to restore open hours lost during earlier budget reductions

But it takes five votes for the city council to take action.

You have shown by your past support that you care deeply about having excellent libraries in your community. We encourage you to exercise your right to express your opinion to the council on all matters, including this one. Council members Jim Compton, Richard Conlin, and Nick Licata seem open to considering the full Steinbrueck/Godden proposal.

Please note that the council will decide on their priorities in the next few days, so if you wish to call or e-mail to encourage them, *do so within the next 48 hours*!

- Compton: XXX@seattle.gov (206) XXX-XXXX
- Conlin: XXX@seattle.gov (206) XXX-XXXX
- Licata: XXX@seattle.gov (206) XXX-XXXX

The cosponsors of the $2.8 million proposal can be reached here:

- Godden: XXX@seattle.gov (206) XXX-XXXX
- Steinbrueck: XXX@seattle.gov (206) XXX-XXXX

Double or triple your impact: send this message along to a friend or two!

Thank you,

Anne Farrell
President
Seattle Public Library Foundation

The discipline and knowledge gained from our community campaign is still relevant today, though the methods for acquiring donors continue to evolve. The use of e-mail as a tool to acquire new donors has become our most cost-efficient way to continue to generate new donors to offset those who stop giving.

To see a sample of a community campaign work plan, see the appendix to this chapter. It is meant to give you a starting place as you develop your plan to build a small donor base.

APPENDIX

Sample of Simplified Work Plan for the Community Campaign

Overall Strategy

Our overall strategy for our three-year community campaign is to front-load scalable fundraising efforts (telefunding, direct mail, e-mail) that will generate the bulk of our community-level gifts. We will leverage broad-reaching awareness efforts to make our fundraising more effective and finish with a grassroots effort to engage as many people and donors as possible from our community.

Campaign Goals and Objectives

Goals—Establish a grassroots partnership with the people of Seattle that ensures an enduring base of donor support for the Seattle Public Library system.

Objectives—Raise gifts toward our $2.5 million goal through small donations while building a sustainable donor base of new users, supporters, and advocates.

Strategies and Key Tactics

Fundraising—Drive new donor acquisition through all appropriate marketing channels and expand ongoing renewal and recapture efforts.

- Build and refine our prospect/donor database for both new donor acquisition and renewal efforts.
- Utilize telefunding and direct mail for both new donor acquisition and renewal.
- Effectively promote benefits of giving to the campaign, and prepare to efficiently fulfill those benefits.

- Design and expand distribution of the quarterly newsletter.
- Look for ways to better serve and inform our new donors through the "tender time" of their life cycle.
- Promote and support library programs as a way to engage and cultivate small donors.
- Develop targeted fundraising and outreach with communities who will support targeted campaigns for special collections, programs, and buildings—as needed.
- Create targeted fundraising appeal to neighborhoods with the most dense donor populations and work with local businesses who want to be affiliated with our project to create more ways to raise funds.

Awareness—Execute a broad-reaching public awareness and information campaign. (The level of sponsor and partner support will drive the scale of each of these tactics.)

- Leverage the My Library creative concept and campaign throughout all foundation marketing activities.
- Develop a clear, simple messaging platform, and deliver it consistently across all media and in all communications.
- Establish media partnerships to maximize campaign exposure.
  - Host a lunch for media company executives, and share our vision and unveil the campaign. All television, radio, outdoor/transit, and print publishers are included. (Note: Instead, we ended up securing one key partnership through direct ask.)
- My Library Community Campaign Kick-Off
  - Create new My Library newsletter, poster series, and website.
- Out-of-branch merchandizing
  - Establish a group of corporate partners, public utilities, and telecommunications companies for in-kind support in the form of $2 for $1 monthly paycheck stuffers and newsletter notices to promote the campaign. (Note: We were not successful in gaining partner support for this.)
  - Secure partnership with major corporate retailers to leverage their retail locations to promote our campaign and giving the retailer the opportunity to be affiliated with such a strong community organization as the library. Design an appropriate promotion directly with each partner, delivering the $2 for $1 message.

Grassroots—Create an active base of support in the local neighborhoods, leveraging construction and other milestones that resonate with the community.

- Identify and implement critical path fundraising activities tied to the opening of a branch in areas where we have had success raising money.
- Support branch openings with foundation presence and leverage the events for donor cultivation (display booth and giveaways promoting foundation).
- Create some sort of activity that energizes the community and gets them thinking about why the library is important to them.
  - The Why I Love My Library Contest

7

Strategies for Seeking External Funding in a Health Science Library

HANNAH F. NORTON, MARY E. EDWARDS,
MICHELE R. TENNANT, AND NINA STOYAN-ROSENZWEIG
Health Science Center Library, University of Florida

BACKGROUND

Librarians at the University of Florida Health Science Center Library have employed an ongoing strategy of seeking both institutional and external grant funding to support outreach events and the development of new services, research and discovery projects, and infrastructure. This strategy began in earnest as the library expanded its traveling exhibit and events program but has also been used to fund a variety of other projects. Our library activities have increasingly relied on grant funding due both to budgetary limitations and to a larger, energized staff with diverse interests for developing new projects. Out of these circumstances has grown a prevailing mind-set of fundraising by looking for local and national grants and funding from campus partners, even in small amounts. Our goals in looking for external funding are to expand the scope of our activities, adding projects that we otherwise would not have the time or resources to pursue, and to increase collaboration with partners within our institution.

This chapter describes a series of specific projects for which we made funding requests and received funding from outside the library, as well as some best practices that we learned about the fundraising process along the way. Table 7.1 summarizes which entities funded each of these projects and whether they are internal or external to the University of Florida (UF).

Table 7.1. Summary of Funded Projects

	Project Name	Funding Source(s)	Funding Amount
Internal Awards			
	Exhibits and Events (four series)	• Center for the Humanities and the Public Sphere • UF Catalyst Fund • UF chapter, Student National Medical Association • UF Genetics Institute • Smathers Libraries Public Relations and Marketing Committee • UF Honors College	$10,200
	Evaluating Tablets for Point of Care Information Service	Smathers Libraries Mini Grant	$1,700
	Internal Medicine Clinic	Gatorade Grant	$29,000
External Awards			
	Exhibits and Events (two series)	National Network of Libraries of Medicine, Southeastern/Atlantic Region	$2,000
	Women's Health Resources Dissemination Outreach Project	National Library of Medicine, NIH Office of Research on Women's Health	$50,000
	Developing an Infrastructure for Information Support for Clinical and Translational Researchers	National Network of Libraries of Medicine, Southeastern/Atlantic Region	$20,000
	Internal Medicine Clinic	National Network of Libraries of Medicine, Southeastern/Atlantic Region	$11,210
	Digitizing Mixed-Media Related to the History of the Health Science Center	National Network of Libraries of Medicine, Southeastern/Atlantic Region	$8,975
	VIVO (amount awarded to UF Libraries)	National Institutes of Health (NIH)	$1,645,845

FUNDING FOR OUTREACH

In order to remain relevant in our context, be a visible presence in our community, and serve the needs of a wide variety of users, the Health Science Center Library (HSCL) has increasingly put an emphasis on broad outreach efforts. While we have historically been well integrated into the educational mission of the colleges we serve, new outreach projects have been aimed at raising awareness of the library's place in the institution and more broadly serving our users' needs. In several cases, such projects would not have been possible without additional funding from outside our library budget.

Exhibits and Events

Given an interest in expanding our offerings for visiting exhibits and associated events in order to better engage our patrons, the members of our exhibits team sought funding from both institutional and external sources. From May 2011 to March 2013, the HSCL hosted four traveling exhibits from the National Library of Medicine (*Frankenstein: Penetrating the Secrets of Nature*; *Opening Doors: Contemporary African American Academic Surgeons*; *Harry Potter's World: Renaissance Science, Magic, and Medicine*; and *A Voyage to Health*).

With each exhibit, we hosted five to eleven related events, ranging from talks by scholars from UF and other institutions to movie screenings to interactive events like suture clinics and receptions with a variety of activities (Auten et al., 2013). Previous exhibits at our library had involved significantly fewer events and no external speakers; thus, the costs were limited to shipping for the exhibit and refreshments at those few events we did host. The exhibits team decided to extend the scope of hosted events with the expectation that this array of events would collectively have a broader appeal among our patrons and the broader university community.

However, bringing in external speakers, screening movies, having refreshments at all events, and having interactive activities significantly increased the cost of putting together an exhibit/events series. In response, we first looked at local opportunities for funding within our institution but outside our particular library.

At UF, the Center for the Humanities and the Public Sphere (CHPS) provides funding for interdisciplinary speakers as long as the series includes a humanities component. This proved a good fit for funding our Frankenstein series, which featured three outside speaker events with English and literature professors, two UF speaker events with biology and bioethics professors, and four movie screenings. Although the funding application itself was not incredibly long (five pages plus an itemized budget), having sufficient information to include in the proposal did require our exhibits team to have event plans and speakers largely finalized at a relatively early juncture (in January, for a May opening). For our Frankenstein series, the CHPS granted the library $2,500, which partly covered the cost of bringing in off-campus speakers. Similarly, for our Harry Potter series, CHPS funding ($2,500) covered expenditures to bring in one of our three external speakers, an English professor. An ancillary benefit to our receiving CHPS funding for these events was that the center advertised each series to their existing mailing list of UF faculty and students with an interest in the humanities, thus broadening our potential audience.

A related local funding opportunity came from the UF Catalyst Fund, a provost-led initiative that supports creative interdisciplinary activities across campus. Again, taking advantage of this opportunity involved developing a funding proposal well in advance of our planned events (in February, for an opening in August of *Harry Potter's World*). In this case, the opportunity to apply for a relatively large amount of funding (up to $25,000) allowed us to think big and begin planning for a robust series with four off-campus speakers, eight movie screenings, three on-campus speaker events, a large opening reception, and film and essay contests. When only $3,500 of our requested $17,500 was awarded, we had to scale back our plans, eliminating one of the external speakers, five of the movie screenings, and the proposed contests.

Despite our receiving less money than we hoped for from this source, this experience taught us that it doesn't hurt to ask for more and later refine priorities when faced with a smaller budget. Additionally, if a project is of interest to a wide audience across the institution, new pockets of money may become available. We received funding directly from the Honors College, whose director knew of our series because of both our Catalyst Fund proposal and an honors course on Harry Potter that the HSCL archivist taught. Figure 7.1 shows librarians' participation in the Harry Potter traveling exhibit.

Hosting a wide variety of exhibits and events has allowed us to build and extend partnerships with additional units on campus by soliciting their assistance in developing event content (i.e., UF faculty giving talks) and jointly funding events. For our *Opening Doors* series, we collaborated with the UF chapter of the Student National Medical Association (SNMA), a student-run organization focused on supporting medical students of color. The SNMA ran a suture clinic for our series, teaching undergraduate and high school students (and the occasional librarian) how to tie surgical knots and sew sutures, and they also hosted a breakfast in conjunction with the keynote speaker's presentation. In another case, we received funding from the UF Genetics Institute for refreshments at two genetics-themed events

Figure 7.1.   Health Science Center Library project team members pose with Harry Potter character cut-outs and the National Library of Medicine traveling exhibit. (Credit: Matthew Daley)

in our Harry Potter series. Of course, not all requests to academic units are successful; although the library also approached the Department of Surgery and Division of Cardiovascular Medicine for *Opening Doors* support, we received no response to these requests.

Another consistent local source of funds for events has been the Public Relations and Marketing Committee (PR&M) of our broader library system, the George A. Smathers Libraries. This fund is available to purchase refreshments for events and promotional materials for libraries at UF. Out of all four of the recent National Library of Medicine (NLM) exhibit/event series held at the HSCL, we have been able to offer refreshments for at least two events due to PR&M funding.

For two of our event series, the HSCL also sought external funding to supplement the cost of the exhibits and events. For *Opening Doors* and *Voyage to Health*, we were successful in obtaining funding from the National Network of Libraries of Medicine Southeastern/Atlantic Region (NN/LM SEA). This funding went to events focused on community health, education, and diversity, aspects that fit well with the priorities of the NN/LM.

Given this plethora of external funding and significant personnel resources invested in the exhibits and events program, it was important for our exhibits team to evaluate the success of the program and assess ways in which to improve our outreach in the future. At each of the four events series, we distributed feedback surveys to event attendees, asking them how they learned about the current event, how they would prefer to learn about library programs in the future, whether their perceptions of the library were affected by the event, and whether they had suggestions for future events. Results of these surveys indicated that attendees were overwhelmingly pleased with the event they attended. Early assessments indicated that attendees preferred to be notified about library events via e-mail announcements, on-campus posters, and newspaper or newsletter articles; therefore, we continued to focus on these means of communication for our subsequent events marketing.

Women's Health Outreach

In considering external funding opportunities, it is important not only to think about core library operations and services but also to think outward and have an open mind as to how you can have an impact beyond your users, such as on the campus or institution as a whole, or even on the community at large. It was this open-minded approach that guided the department when we were approached about a Women's Health Resources Dissemination Outreach Project funding opportunity from NLM and the National Institutes of Health (NIH) Office of Research on Women's Health.

Our department chair had successfully competed for, and received, NLM and NIH funding previously and was approached about putting together a plan for an existing Women's Health Resources Dissemination Outreach Project contract. Once the initial request for proposal submission was received, the project team was formed quickly and worked to turn out a full, forty-nine-page proposal (including a list of collaborators and eight letters of support) in fifteen working days. While this very short time frame may seem daunting, and it was a challenge, being flexible and willing to accept opportunities is crucial to building variety in funding sources. Agreeing to draft a proposal for a rather comprehensive project with a short turnaround time could be considered risky, but various factors helped facilitate the process and ultimately ensure our success.

One of the key elements of our ability to create a well-received project proposal was the HSCL's long-standing and robust liaison program (Tennant et al., 2001; Tennant et al., 2006). The liaison program cultivates librarians' relationships with their users, especially faculty and clinicians. It was those well-developed collaborations that allowed us to respond so quickly to a request to submit a proposal. The request for funding focused on outreach and collaboration, and, toward that end, the funding agencies required that successfully funded institutions develop and work closely with collaborators and partners. In order to compile a list of willing partners and solicit letters of support and collaboration, we leveraged the existing relationships of the project team members and our department as a whole.

The final project proposal was accepted by the funding source, and we were awarded the amount of $50,000 to implement the project. Components of the project included instructional sessions in which we introduced the topic of sex and gender differences in health and promoted the Women's Health Resources portal, a series of collaboration workshops using the CoLAB Planning Series® to facilitate discussion and networking of researchers interested in the topic, the addition of resources on the topic to our collection, and an open access publishing fund to help promote access to research on this topic.

Considering that the time line for the project was short and the workload for the proposal was heavy, you may ask yourself why it was important for the library to participate in this project. Working with our partners to help promote the goals of the funding agencies allowed us to further develop those existing collaborations and also reach out to form new collaborations with groups outside our normal purview, including UF's Center for Women's Studies and Gender Research. While helping to create a name for our library and expand our institutional contacts was an admirable outcome, receiving funding for the project had other, more pragmatic outcomes. External funding from the contract allowed the library to expand its collections and services without tapping into an increasingly tight budget. Additionally, the contract provided funding for team members to attend and present on the project at regional and national conferences.

FUNDING FOR RESEARCH AND DISCOVERY

As librarians seek to participate in the research and discovery process, potential obstacles can include funding for such projects. In order to financially support research and discovery-related projects, it can be important to search for and utilize alternative funding sources, including grants.

Mini Grants

While grants external to an institution can be of great benefit, many institutions or libraries offer internal awards as well. For example, our library system has a program of Mini Grants, which are small grants designed to help librarians gain experience in the grant application process from conception through administration. The maximum award for a Mini Grant is $5,000. To select grantees, the library has a Grants Management Committee, which evaluates each project and recommends to the libraries' dean whether funds are deserved. In addition to helping librarians develop experience with grant writing, these awards can help supplement research and discovery projects within the library. In the past five years, the HSCL has received several Mini Grants, which we have used to fund various projects within the library, including those related to research and development.

One project in particular illustrates how internal grant funding can seed research in new areas. The project, Evaluating Tablets for Point-of-Care Information Services, was conceived to study how the use of mobile technology (tablets) impacts the provision of information services during clinical rounds. The total award amounted to approximately $1,700. Grant funds were used to purchase two tablet devices (one Apple and one Android device) and cases for the respective devices. During the course of the project, librarians used the tablets to search for information while participating on rounds with the Department of Pediatrics in support of evidence-based medicine. The tablets were evaluated for ease of use and applicability to the clinical setting. Results from the evaluation were shared at regional and national meetings, which helped contribute to the knowledge in the area of mobile technology for clinical support. The tablets are still used when librarians round in the clinical setting. A best practices recommendation is that you explore all sources of grant funding (internal and external to your institution), no matter how small the amount of available funds.

Clinical and Translational Science Research Support

In order to provide appropriate services and resources, librarians and other information professionals seek to understand the information needs of their clients. Library users have diverse information needs based on their roles, such as student versus faculty member, clinician versus researcher, or dentist versus nurse. The area of clinical and translational science research (CTS) has developed to speed the translation of bench research into use in the clinic and the community. CTS researchers are a diverse group, including basic scientists, clinicians and clinical researchers, journalists, educators, community engagement professionals, and others. Because CTS strategies are becoming so foundational to biomedical research, it is useful for librarians and other information providers to understand the information needs of this specific population. CTS Awards (CTSAs) from the NIH provide funds to the institution to support the CTS infrastructure. UF was awarded its CTSA in July 2009.

To support UF's fledgling Clinical and Translational Science Institute (CTSI), librarians at the HSCL in 2011 applied for and received a separate

$20,000 NN/LM SEA CTSA infrastructure pilot project grant titled Developing an Infrastructure for Information Support for Clinical and Translational Researchers. The general, bioinformatics, and data management needs of these researchers were explored through researcher surveys; data management needs interviews were also performed.

Although the primary purpose of this grant was to learn about the information needs of this population so that the library could devise strategies and innovative services to meet the information needs of and benefit CTS researchers, there were also benefits afforded the library. Prior to submission of the grant, two activities—assessing research impact and assisting with systematic reviews—were hypothesized as being useful to CTS researchers. However, the HSCL librarians were not trained in either aspect. The successful grant proposal funded two systematic review assistance experts to travel to Gainesville and provide training to all librarians at the HSCL and its satellite Borland Library. The grant also funded five librarians to travel to learn about serving the information needs of clinical and translational science researchers, as well as assessing research impact and library-based assistance for the CTSA renewals.

While developing services specifically for the researchers affiliated with UF's newly funded CTSI had been on the HSCL's radar since the institute's inception, it had been difficult to find the time for needs assessment and planning given the wide variety of client information needs and projects in which the library was involved. Once the project was grant-funded, moving this work to the top of the library's priority list was easily justified (and, in fact, essential).

Supporting Consumer Health in an Internal Medicine Clinic

Another area of growth for the HSCL has been in promoting consumer health and partnering with UF faculty and students as they work on research related to patient education and expanding health literacy. In particular, two of our librarians have been able to spend dedicated time on a patient-focused project in a UF internal medicine clinic due to a series of funding opportunities.

The project, initially funded by an NN/LM SEA Express Planning and Assessment Award ($5,209), involves having a librarian embedded in the clinic on a weekly basis and available to help patients in the waiting room develop questions for their doctors and find appropriate consumer health information to discuss with their doctors. At the end of the six-month implementation funded by NN/LM, the Consumer Health & Community Outreach librarian and her internal medicine physician collaborator were interested in extending the project, and they applied for Gatorade support, specifically available to faculty in the UF College of Medicine. The

$29,000 award funded the librarian's time in the clinic as well as computing equipment and expanded that time from one afternoon per week to one afternoon and one morning per week.

Again, given the success of the project and the desire among participants to continue it even with changes in personnel (both the librarian and the physician partner retiring from UF), the liaison librarian to the Division of General Internal Medicine was recruited, as was a new physician collaborator, and additional funding ($6,000) was received from the NN/LM SEA through an Express Outreach Follow-Up Award. This most recent iteration of the project, currently still in effect, expands the outreach efforts of the library through an introduction of the Information Prescription pad for physicians to use in referring patients to MedlinePlus and/or further library assistance between their clinic visits.

In all three of the fundraising activities related to discovery (rounding, the CTSI, and internal medicine), the process started with the clear goal of developing services for client groups, which to that point had not been addressed by the HSCL. Staff time was initially spent thoroughly researching trends and innovative services through the literature, working closely with the libraries' grants manager, and then finally writing the grants. The HSCL discovery efforts have led to enhanced collaborations with clients and the development of new services:

- Two librarians now round regularly with Pediatrics, utilizing the tablets that were secured by the grant.
- The CTSI's administration was actively involved in the dissemination of the needs assessments and is eagerly awaiting data analysis. New services such as systematic review assistance, data management, and expanded bioinformatics services have been created.
- The Internal Medicine clinic work continues with an expansion to new personnel and the development of services for patients between clinic visits.

FUNDING FOR INFRASTRUCTURE

A final area in which the HSCL has sought and received funding from outside the library is that of expanding and modernizing elements of library and campus infrastructure. Although infrastructure is generally an ongoing cost to libraries and their parent institutions, specific infrastructure-related projects may still be attractive to potential funders, including projects that provide ongoing benefit with one-time funding and projects that offer innovation and widespread value.

Digitization of Archival Materials

The issue of migrating media from obsolete formats to currently readable formats is increasingly a focal point for archivists. It requires developing policies on prioritizing materials to migrate based on such characteristics as what materials are currently in demand, which are most likely to be used soon if available, and which are most in danger of being permanently lost through deterioration. Of course, how many items can be transferred depends on how much money is available. Electronic media migration plans are, therefore, largely dependent on available funds, for both in-house and external migration services. Many long-term collection digitization plans include not just scanning paper media but also ensuring that electronic media can be accessed and preserved.

Sometimes, however, the scenario is further complicated by lack of information on currently unreadable media, so it is unclear which items will be of interest and which will be less significant to the main archives mission. At the HSCL, external funding sources to cover digitization were important to catalog and describe the multimedia portion of the Health Science Center (HSC) Archives collection. Thus, the HSCL archivist is always on the lookout for funding sources that could support projects digitizing electronic media. When the NN/LM SEA call for proposals included potential grants for digitization of electronic media, it was a perfect fit for digitizing part of the film collection that included reel-to-reel film, one-inch film, and a variety of other media collected over a period of fifty years. The success of the grant made it possible to digitize parts of the collection that could then be uploaded to the libraries' digital collections.

The total collection of media contained several hundred multimedia items of this mix that were created largely within the HSC for publicity or educational purposes. These materials came from different colleges, the media and publicity office, and administrative units in the HSC. They included videos created to train students in the patient interview; descriptions of new treatments; descriptions and tours of new facilities; records of student activities; clips recording important events in the history of the HSC; and a range of other materials that documented the growth and development of the HSC, educational approaches, and development of clinical treatments. To make these valuable institutional resources more accessible, the HSC archivist was successful in receiving an Express Digitization and Conservation Award from the NN/LM SEA for the project, Digitizing Mixed Media Related to the History of the Health Science Center ($8,974). This grant funding covered digitization of over a hundred Umatic tapes, cassettes, and reel-to-reel audiotapes.

Given the importance of ensuring access to older digital collections, there are a number of grants available for libraries and archives. Various government and foundation websites list potential digitization grant sources, including the Federal Depository Library (http://registry.fdlp.gov/grants); Library of Congress (www.loc.gov/preservation/about/foundtn-grants.pdf); National Archives (www.archives.gov/nhprc/announcement/); and Visual Resources Association (www.vraweb.org/organization/committees/digitalinit/imlsgrants.html). Some of these grant sources cover electronic records; others cover other types of records such as photographs and paper records.

Enhancing Researcher Discovery and Collaboration with VIVO

VIVO is an online Semantic Web researcher discovery and collaboration tool that was initially developed by the Cornell University Library. Through a major grant funded via the American Recovery and Reinvestment Act, UF and six collaborating institutions expanded, enhanced, and disseminated this tool, with the HSCL and another UF library (Marston Science Library) playing key roles in implementation and adoption in the first two years of the project. Further information on VIVO can be found at www.vivoweb.org/.

The VIVO project was quite a departure for the HSCL—both in the scope of the work and in the size of the total award to participating collaborators (over $12.2 million, with over $1.6 million to UF libraries). The HSCL's participation in the project was also unusual for us at that time in that it required our librarians to work in cross-disciplinary, multi-institutional teams with other information professionals, IT specialists, programmers, computer scientists, marketing and advertising specialists, educators, and others (Garcia-Milian et al., 2013). The library's participation in such a large and complex project was somewhat risky, but at the same time it offered us a unique opportunity to be involved in an institution-level informatics project.

The librarians at the HSCL derived numerous benefits from the project, both intellectual and tangible. Work on VIVO presented our library staff with opportunities for professional growth and development in the areas of project management, semantic technologies, outreach, marketing, and working in those cross-disciplinary, multi-institutional teams. We developed closer professional relationships with our clients through our outreach and educational activities. From a practical standpoint, the HSCL received salary savings for the VIVO-related work of the project team—enough that the team was able to hire a temporary full-time "VIVO Backfill Librarian." This librarian worked out so well that at the end of the grant period, as part of a general restructuring of staff, HSCL administration found the funds to keep this librarian. The grant also provided numerous opportunities for presentation on VIVO at local and national conferences, as well as the funding to send HSCL librarians to make these presentations.

While VIVO was a complex and challenging project for HSCL librarians and outside our usual scope of activities, our participation broadened our skill sets and our mind-sets and helped the HSCL evolve such that seeking funding is now part of our professional DNA. It is no coincidence that all of the fundraising and grant activities described above occurred after the HSCL had been involved in the VIVO project.

NEXT STEPS AND LESSONS LEARNED

Given the success of these grant-funded projects, HSCL librarians plan to continue to investigate new funding opportunities related to library and institutional needs and priorities, particularly those that allow us to build on and expand interdisciplinary partnerships. We also plan to continue work on the projects described above that were started with grant funding. Our experience receiving funding from a wide variety of organizations outside our library for a wide variety of projects has taught us many lessons about fundraising. As such, we offer the following "best practice" advice to other libraries with an interest in expanding the scope and sources of their grant-funded projects.

1. Collaboration is key.
2. A thorough understanding of library and institutional priorities; research, educational, and clinical landscapes; and other aspects of the environment is essential when considering fundraising of any nature.
3. Find a funding agency that matches well with your library and institution's needs and priorities, and then closely align your proposal to the agency/program.
4. Needs assessment, project evaluation, and findings dissemination are key—but often neglected—components of the grant application process. Paying close attention to these areas when writing the grant will increase the likelihood of funding.
5. Think about ancillary (but legitimate) activities that can be funded by the grant and that will benefit the library—such as salary savings, travel to conferences to present results, and training.
6. Think small—small grants can serve as demonstration projects that can then lead to larger funding opportunities.
7. Think big—librarians are well positioned to coordinate and/or contribute to large-scale team projects.
8. Keep a wish list of priorities, and be on the lookout for matching funding agencies.
9. Check to see what has been recently funded by agencies in your library's areas of interest; this can spark ideas.

ACKNOWLEDGMENTS

Exhibit and Events

This project has been funded in whole or in part with federal funds from the National Library of Medicine, National Institutes of Health, under contract no. HHS-N-276-2011-00004-C. The events described were sponsored in part by the UF Center for the Humanities and the Public Sphere with support from the Yavitz and Rothman Funds, the UF chapter of the Student National Medical Association, the UF Catalyst Fund, the UF Genetics Institute, the UF Honors College, the Alachua County Library District, and the George A. Smathers Libraries Public Relations and Marketing Committee.

Women's Health Outreach

This project has been funded in part with federal funds from the National Library of Medicine, National Institutes of Health, under contract no. HHS-N-316-2012-00028-W.

Evaluating Tablets for Point-of-Care Information Services

This project has been funded in whole or in part with Mini Grant funds from the George A. Smathers Libraries.

Clinical and Translational Science Research Support

This project has been funded in whole or in part with federal funds from the National Library of Medicine, National Institutes of Health, under contract no. HHS-N-276-2011-00004-C.

Supporting Consumer Health in an Internal Medicine Clinic

This project has been funded in whole or in part with federal funds from the National Library of Medicine, National Institutes of Health, under contract no. HHS-N-276-2011-00004-C, and continued with Gatorade Research Funds through the Department of Medicine at the University of Florida College of Medicine.

Digitization of Archival Materials

This project has been funded in whole or in part with federal funds from the National Library of Medicine, National Institutes of Health, under contract no. HHS-N-276-2011-00004-C.

Enhancing Researcher Discovery and Collaboration with VIVO

This project was funded by the National Institutes of Health, U24 RR029822, "VIVO: Enabling National Networking of Scientists."

REFERENCES

Auten, Beth, Hannah F. Norton, Michele R. Tennant, Mary E. Edwards, Nina C. Stoyan-Rosenzweig, and Matthew Daley. 2013. "Using NLM Exhibits and Events to Engage Library Users and Reach the Community." *Medical Reference Services Quarterly* 32, no. 3 (July–September): 266–89.

Garcia-Milian, Rolando, Hannah F. Norton, and Beth Auten, et al. 2013. "Librarians as Part of Cross-Disciplinary, Multi-Institutional Team Projects: Experiences from the VIVO Collaboration." *Science & Technology Libraries* 32, no. 2: 160–75.

Tennant, Michele R., Linda C. Butson, Michelle E. Rezeau, Prudence J. Tucker, Marian E. Boyle, and Greg Clayton. 2001. "Customizing for Clients: Developing a Library Liaison Program from Need to Plan." *Bulletin of the Medical Library Association* 89, no. 1 (January): 8–20.

Tennant, Michele R., Tara T. Cataldo, Pamela Sherwill-Navarro, and Rae Jesano. 2006. "Evaluation of a Liaison Librarian Program: Client and Liaison Perspectives." *Journal of the Medical Library Association* 94, no. 4 (October): 402–9, e201–4.

8

Developing the Potential of a Library's Board

Christina Muracco
Smithsonian Libraries

THE ROLE OF THE LIBRARY'S BOARD OF DIRECTORS

Developing and maintaining an effective library board of directors requires a significant investment of time and staff resources. However, a well-developed board will likely be the library's strongest advocate and its largest donor. While board roles and functions vary among institutions, ultimately board involvement will revolve around raising awareness of the library's services and resources and raising funds to support the library (see Figure 8.1).

This chapter will give you some reference tools, ideas, and best practices to create a board of directors for your library or refine the roles of your existing board. Consider the following when developing a staffing plan for your board:

- Who will plan and staff your board meetings?
- Who will assist the board in planning and hosting events?
- How often will you update the board on library news and fundraising progress?
- Who is the board's main staff contact for questions or scheduling visits, tours, or appointments?

All libraries are different. The audiences they serve, their sizes, the size of the staff, and their missions are all unique. For this reason, not all library boards will be alike. How do you envision a board advancing your library's mission? Fundraising and advocacy are common themes for a nonprofit board's mission statement. Clarifying the mission and vision of your board will also give members and prospective board members a sense of how you

Figure 8.1.   A board's help with fundraising is crucial to sustain busy libraries like the National Museum of Natural History Library. (Credit: Courtesy of Smithsonian Libraries)

expect them to help your cause. The following websites have tools to help you articulate your board's mission and vision:

GuideStar, www.guidestar.org
The NonProfit Times, www.thenonprofittimes.com

Before forming your board, or when you are ready to make changes to your board, a good first step is to start building or reviewing your bylaws. Bylaws are the basic foundation of your board's operations. Your bylaws should include the mission and vision of your board and clarify your expectations of your board. Bylaws should address the following areas.

Governance and Structure

- Address the general purpose of your board.
- Be clear who has the authority to modify and approve your bylaws.
- Note whether your board serves solely an advisory capacity or whether members have fiduciary responsibility.
- Determine the maximum size of your board.
- List your board's officers, terms, roles, and how they are elected.

- Bear in mind that board officers often include chair, vice chair, secretary, and/or treasurer.
- Ask yourself what the provisions for ex-officio, emeritus, alumni, and/or honorary board members will be.

Board Committees

- Standing Committees—State your standing committees and their purposes. Standing committees are often an executive committee and a nominating committee, depending on the size of your board. A small board may operate as a committee of the whole for a time. Address the purpose, roles, responsibilities, and membership of each standing committee.
- Ad Hoc Committees—Address if and when ad hoc committees may be formed and who approves their creation. Address the purpose, roles, responsibilities, and membership of each current ad hoc committee.

Board Committee Membership

- Who appoints a board member to a committee?
- Do all board members need to be on a committee?
- What expectations are there of the committee?
- Will the committees have chairs? If so, what are the expectations of the chairs?
- What are the terms of service for the committee members?

Identification of Board Candidates

List what criteria board members should use when considering a board candidate. Qualifications to consider when vetting a person for board membership could include the following:

- Has this person demonstrated a desire to serve institutions like your library?
- Is this person financially capable of supporting your library on an annual basis, as well as participating in long-term financial and campaign projects?
- Does this person have unique skills or knowledge that would help your library achieve its mission?
- Is this person willing to commit the time to participate on your board?
- Does this candidate have a particular subject area of interest that is addressed by your library's resources?
- Will this person's profile in the community support your mission?

- Does the candidate have potential or perceived conflicts of interest? Can they be addressed?

The Nominating Process

- How are board candidates identified?
- Is there a vetting process?
- Does the board vote on new candidates? If so, how many members must be present for a vote to be held?
- Is there an orientation process for new members?

Calendar of Meetings

- How often and for how long will the board meet?
- Where will the board meet?
- How are board members given notice of a meeting?
- What are the procedures for canceling a meeting?

Terms of Board Service

- How long is a term of service?
- How many terms can a board member serve?
- What are the resignation and termination procedures?

Board Member Expectations and Responsibilities

Sample board member expectations and responsibilities include those listed here:

- Prepare for, attend, and contribute to all board and assigned committee meetings.
- Take responsibility for becoming educated about your library.
- Identify and present new board member candidates.
- Advocate and promote the events and activities of your library.
- Contribute financially to the success of your library and its mission.

Strong bylaws serve you well through difficult situations and when managing board member expectations. Bylaws should be in place before your first board meeting, and reviewing and refreshing the bylaws can be a task assigned to one of your board's committees. Sample bylaw templates can be found online on websites such as the following:

Foundation Center, http://foundationcenter.org
Grant Space, http://grantspace.org
Nolo Law, www.nolo.com

Best Practices: Successful boards frequently evaluate their priorities, committees, and membership to adapt to the changing needs of the libraries they support.

ESTABLISHING A BOARD THAT'S RIGHT FOR YOUR LIBRARY

Attracting Board Members Who Work for You

Every library has compelling reasons for potential board members to get involved. Reasons often include prestige, a great community cause, networking, and a passion for the mission of your organization. Whatever the case, developing an articulate, concise, and consistent way for you and your board members to tout your library will be essential to recruiting the right board members.

Best Practices: Engage board members and staff in an exercise to develop your elevator speech. An elevator speech is a thirty- to sixty-second summary of your organization. A board member's elevator speech to a prospective board member should quickly convey the mission of your library, why your library is worthy of support, and why they got involved.

Clarifying Board Member Expectations

A board handbook can be used to clarify board member expectations before a candidate joins your board. A handbook can also be used to welcome and orient new board members and serve as a reference tool for current board members (see Figure 8.2).

A comprehensive handbook should include the following information:

- A brief history of your organization
- Your library's strategic plan
- Your mission and vision
- A staff organization chart
- Staff contact information
- A guide on how to use library resources
- A campus and/or library locations map

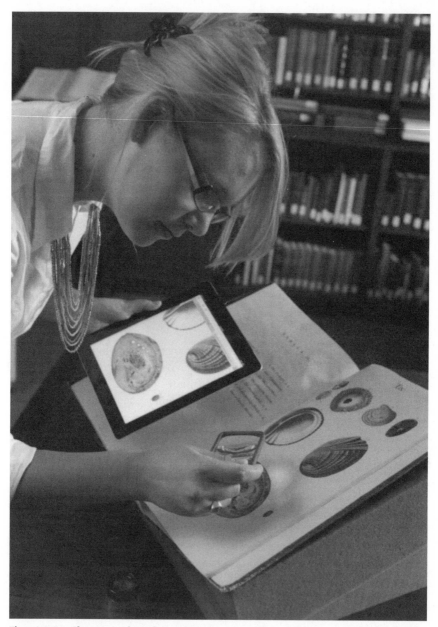

Figure 8.2.   Show your board members how to utilize the resources of your library. Shown here, the online Biodiversity Heritage Library. (Credit: Courtesy of Smithsonian Libraries)

The handbook should outline board member expectations and review fundraising and campaign-related information. It will also include your board's bylaws and contact and bio information for your current board members (some organizations include an alumni/emeritus board member directory as well). As the handbook is revised, new versions should be sent out to current board members. A well-written handbook can be used in response to a board member's exclamation of "I didn't sign up for that!"

Best Practices: After having a conversation with a board candidate about joining your board, leave the handbook with them to review board-membership expectations and your library's priorities.

Recruiting, Retaining, and Term Limits for Board Members

Recruiting the right board members is essential for building a board and critical for maintaining the success of an established board. Recruiting members with skills that can help advance your cause will increase engagement and ultimately increase their investment in your organization. To narrow your recruiting focus, think about the board's main priorities and what skill sets you need to accomplish these tasks.

- Do you need to raise the visibility of your library? Why not think about recruiting someone in the marketing or public relations field to help?
- Does your library have a new science collection you'd like to promote? Why not recruit someone with a science background to increase your network?
- Are you interested in increasing alumni support for your business school collection? Consider approaching alumni in business who can understand and attest to the importance of the collection.
- Is raising money a priority? Why not look for someone with fundraising experience?

Filling out a matrix of skill sets will help you home in on the right candidates. Existing board members are vital to recruiting new members, so sharing your skill-set needs with the board will help them tap their networks more effectively. Table 8.1 is an example of a skill-set matrix.

Table 8.1. Example of a Skill-Set Matrix

EXPERTISE	BOARD MEMBER #1	BOARD MEMBER #2	BOARD MEMBER #3
ARTS			
BUSINESS ADMINISTRATION			
COMMUNITY VISIBILITY			
EDUCATION			
FINANCE			
FUNDRAISING			
INFORMATION TECHNOLOGY			
LIBRARY			
MARKETING OR PUBLIC RELATIONS			
STRATEGIC PLANNING			

The Recruiting Process

A structured annual recruiting and orientation process will save you time and resources. Consider starting a new class of board members at the same time every year. Using an annual recruiting and orientation model will provide your board with a reliable time line to submit candidates. It will also give new members a consistent orientation experience and build camaraderie within the class. An annual process will save you from replicating the recruiting and orientation process several times a year. An example of a recruiting and orientation time line is shown in Table 8.2.

Have your board members complete nomination forms along with names of people they would like the board to consider as candidates. Nomination forms should give the nominating committee an overview of why the person should be considered for the board. Along with basic contact information, a nomination form could address the following:

- Has the candidate expressed an interest in your library?
- Has the candidate expressed an interest in serving on your library's board?

Table 8.2.   Example of a Recruiting and Orientation Time Line

TIME LINE	RECRUITING AND ORIENTATION TASKS FOR BOARD	RECRUITING AND ORIENTATION TASKS FOR STAFF
MARCH–MAY	Board submits names and bios of candidates to Nominating Committee. Nominating Committee determines which candidates should be contacted to pursue board membership.	Staff conducts research on board candidates.
JUNE– SEPTEMBER	Nominating Committee presents the candidates to the board, and the board votes on the nominations.	Staff contacts candidates and extends an invitation to visit library and meet selected board members.
OCTOBER– DECEMBER	Approved new board members are invited to participate on committee conference calls to determine which committee they would like to join.	
JANUARY– FEBRUARY	Board approves new board member orientation program.	Staff plans orientation program to kick off new board members' terms.

- Do you anticipate that the candidate will be a contributor of funds to your library?
- What network(s) and or community contact(s) can the candidate introduce to your library?
- What skill set or background does the candidate possess that will be relevant to the needs of your library?

Best Practices: During board meetings, be sure your nominating committee reminds the board what stage of the recruiting process you are in so that they can participate accordingly.

Orienting Board Members

Providing an orientation program for new board members will educate and introduce them to your staff members. An orientation program could include the following:

- An overview and history of your organization
- An outline of your organization's finances and administration

- Current organizational initiatives
- Fundraising goals and priorities
- Tours of special collections and other locations or branches (see Figure 8.3)
- Lunch or dinner with board members

Best Practices: Orientation programs work well just before a new member's first board meeting. Timing orientation in this way gives a new member a sense of confidence in their knowledge of the organization and prepares them to meet the full board.

Applying Term Limits

Applying term limits is a good way to keep your board dynamic. Though it's hard to lose faithful and dedicated members, term limits can give members a chance to review their commitment to your library. However, a term-renewal clause for exceptional members can always be added to your bylaws. In tougher scenarios, enforcing term limits is usually the best way to move ineffective or disruptive members off your board.

Figure 8.3.   Get your new board members excited to promote your library by arranging special tours. Shown here, a behind-the-scenes tour educates board members about Botanica Magnifica, a unique folio by Jonathan Singer in the Smithsonian Libraries. (Credit: Courtesy of Smithsonian Libraries)

Evaluating Board Members

How will you hold your board accountable? Some organizations find board "report cards" helpful. Report cards are simply an annual review of a board member's contributions to your organization. The board member expectations you developed for your bylaws can be your guide to track participation. A report card can be filled out by staff and reviewed with a board member during a one-on-one meeting. Alternatively, board members can submit their annual participation by way of a self-evaluation. Self-evaluations can be discussed one-on-one, reviewed by the library director, or analyzed by the executive committee. Sample board "report cards" and self-evaluations can be found on the following websites:

National Council of Nonprofits, www.councilofnonprofits.org
Nonprofit Resource Center, www.nprcenter.org

Another way to stay on top of your board's health and welfare is to create a board stewardship committee. A board stewardship committee could create and administer board member surveys and conduct exit interviews. A committee like this could take charge of complaints and provide suggestions for remedies.

Best Practices: Add a board section to your website that includes board member profiles and current activities and events. Offer to submit press releases announcing new board members to their local papers. This will steward your new board member and give your organization some publicity. Recognize board member contributions, both financial and otherwise, during board meetings or in your regular communications to the board.

Establishing Board Committees

Developing standing and ad hoc or task-driven committees to engage and take advantage of the talents and interests of your board will boost their productivity and overall effectiveness. Each committee should have a chair responsible for calling the committee's meetings, setting the agendas, and reporting on the committee's progress to the full board. Articulating your standing committees, such as the executive committee, which will govern your board, and the nominating committee, which will drive the recruiting and orientation process, will be your first step. The roles of standing committees should be outlined in your bylaws. As you establish ad hoc committees, consider the following:

- What are your organization's priorities?
- How do you envision the board advancing your mission?
- Where do you need the most help?

Your board's committees should evolve to suit the changing needs of your library. If your library is a little-known secret in your community, consider a marketing committee to help raise your profile. If you're looking for ways to engage your current donors and build your pipeline of prospective donors, consider a donor engagement committee. If you're struggling to articulate your strategic plan, create a committee to help you think through it. A public programming committee could help with your outreach efforts. A technology committee could help you build your network in the IT community. Not only will board members engaged on committees like these be able to help you with their time and efforts, but they might also be able to connect you to in-kind donations for services like marketing, public relations, website development, and so forth.

Best Practices: Assigning at least one staff member to each committee will allow you to take advantage of staff skill sets and give the board exposure to a diverse range of staff. This also ensures that no one staff member is responsible for managing all of the committees.

Holding Board Meetings

Board meeting formats will vary depending on the structure and preference of your board. Some boards prefer committees to meet face to face during the board meeting. Other boards find that committees are more productive when they meet outside the board meeting. Some factors to consider when planning the format of your meetings include the following:

- Will there be regular staff presentations?
- Will your meetings include a tour or lecture?
- Will there be time for board discussions?
- Will there be social events?
- Will there be ways to engage spouses?

Board members should receive the meeting agenda along with the last board meeting's minutes at least one week before the meeting. Providing the board with materials in advance gives you more time to focus on the future rather than rehashing what happened at the last meeting. Items to go over in every board meeting include:

- An update from the director of your library
- Committee reports
- Minutes approval

Best Practices: Set your board meeting schedule at least one year in advance to achieve greater attendance. For example, plan to meet the first Thursday and Friday of October, March, and June. Survey the board annually to see whether the timing, dates, and format of your meetings are working for them. Remember, your board members are volunteers—scheduling some time for fun, networking, and socializing should always be included in the agenda.

Fundraising and Campaigns . . . Is My Board on Board?

There are many different scenarios that can arise when an organization starts to emphasize fundraising. Ideally, the chair and the vice chair of your board should be your greatest advocates. With their help, you should be able to assure the board that fundraising is a good idea for your library and should be one of the board's highest priorities.

Your chair and vice chair should be able to help you institute a mandatory annual gift (or "dues") for board members. Establishing an annual gift policy will help your board become more invested in your fundraising goals. For example, many libraries desperately need discretionary funds. Outlining your past use of discretionary funds and what you *will not* be able to accomplish this year unless the funds are acquired can make the case that annual board gifts be designated as such. Other organizations find that board members bond over funding a special annual project each year. What is most important is getting your board into the habit of giving and fundraising (see Figure 8.4).

Sometimes advisory boards are created to do just that: give advice. Shifting a board of this kind into a fundraising board can take some time, and you could lose some members. The best way to convert this type of board is to emphasize 100 percent board participation in the campaign rather than attempt to coerce board members into a making a major gift. As advisors, board members should realize the importance of fundraising and make an effort to be part of your library's success.

Ultimately, working with your board to develop campaign goals and tools will make them feel more invested in fundraising. It's likely that your average donor profile will be represented by some of your board members; and hopefully some of your board members will be your best donors. As you develop fundraising materials, it is essential to solicit their feedback and ideas.

Another way to ease your board into fundraising is to give them progress updates. As they become invested in your successes and challenges, the

Figure 8.4. A successful fundraising event supported by the Smithsonian Libraries Advisory Board. (Credit: Elizabeth O'Brien/Courtesy of the Smithsonian Libraries)

process will become more exciting. Fundraising updates will also keep your goals fresh in their minds and make them more likely to feel confident in sharing the news with their networks. Be sure your board is the first to know if your fundraising priorities change.

Not every board member will be an amazing fundraiser, and that is normal. Clarify your fundraising expectations, and offer specific ways they can help. There are plenty of opportunities to employ those members who don't want to get involved in solicitations. Some ways to engage board members in your fundraising efforts include those listed below:

- Supplying a list of prospects. Work with a board member on appropriate ways to engage these prospects. A letter? A personal visit? Attend an event?
- Hosting events. Successful events can be anything from hosting a small group of prospects for coffee or cocktails to underwriting a gala.
- Making an introduction for you to visit a potential major donor.
- Reviewing solicitation letters, and participating in solicitations.

Many fundraising consultants offer special training and workshops for nonprofit board members. Classes can vary from major gifts and campaign lessons to simply learning how to leverage their networks.

Best Practices: Have a committee of the board dedicated to fundraising. If you have a large board, have one committee dedicated to helping with major gifts and another committee to focus on annual giving and ways to build your donor pipeline. Ask the committees to share their success stories and challenges with the board.

Focusing Board Priorities on Library Priorities

"My board has gone wild and has its own initiatives; anarchy has ensued" is not a complaint many people envision when putting together a board, but unfortunately sometimes difficult situations arise. Clarifying board member expectations and having clear bylaws can help you prevent trying circumstances, but sometimes they are unavoidable. Some common scenarios include the following:

- Your board wants you to accept a gift that is not suitable for your collection.
- Your board wants to move forward with a board candidate you feel is unsuitable.
- The board criticizes your leadership or management style.

A strong board chair and executive committee can help you with many of these issues. Board-member-to-board-member conversations oftentimes can restore peace and productivity. Engaging an outside consultant to speak to the board or having someone else from your staff reiterate your point of view can also shed light on your perspective. Transparency and frequent communication will help you build the confidence and trust of your board.

Best Practices: Keep your staff apprised of the work the board is doing. A summary of minutes or highlights of the board meeting is usually sufficient. Engage your staff with the board whenever possible. Remember, the board has varied interests, so exposure to staff from different areas of your organization might spark interest in unexpected ways.

FINAL THOUGHTS

Keeping your board interested and engaged in your library is vital to their success. Generate excitement by sharing your hopes and aspirations with board members, and remind them of the progress you have made with their help. An annual or biannual board survey can keep you apprised of what is working for your board. A survey gives board members an opportunity to anonymously share feedback about their experience on the board and with your library. The survey could include questions on the following topics:

- Ease in articulating the history, mission, vision, and strategic plan of your library
- Understanding your library's budget and finance operations
- Knowledge of the board's roles and responsibilities
- Effectiveness of board meetings
- Effectiveness of board committee structure
- Understanding fundraising priorities

Use feedback from the survey to improve and refine your board. Before board members cycle off the board, be sure to offer them an exit interview. An exit interview will shed insight on their experience and give you an opportunity to improve the experiences of current and future board members.

Best Practices: Keep former board members involved in your library by engaging them on a board alumni group or by asking them to participate on a board committee. Continue sending them your board's alumni group news updates and invite them to special events. If your alumni group is large enough, consider planning special activities and communications just for them.

In time, the resources and efforts invested in your library's board should reward your library with a sophisticated group of advocates and donors to champion your cause. Best of luck with your efforts!

9

Quick Wins in Planned Giving for Libraries: Documenting Simple Bequests

KARLENE NOEL JENNINGS

The College of William and Mary

Unlike other chapters in this book, this one is not about working with a specific donor, campaign priority, or case for support. Rather, it is a donor strategy to maximize simple bequests for your library. It allows your library to further its mission by increasing its long-term donations. Many larger libraries already have active planned giving programs; the purpose of this chapter is to serve as a reminder that basic tools can often be the most successful over the long haul for libraries and other nonprofit organizations.

Recently, while preparing our library for its next comprehensive campaign, I took the opportunity to review the library's historic list of its top 10, 50, and 100 donors. These lists were dominated by individuals who included the library in their estate plans (some gave substantial gifts in their lifetimes as well). Our library is not unique, as this trend happens at many libraries—public, academic, and special. As a development officer, my job (and my passion) is making it as easy as possible for the donors I work with to achieve their philanthropic dreams. This includes planned giving opportunities.

According to the Association of Fundraising Professionals, planned giving is "a systematic effort to identify and cultivate a person, for the purpose of generating a major gift, that is structured and that integrates sound personal, financial, and estate-planning concepts with the prospect's plan for lifetime or testamentary giving. A planned gift has tax implications and is often transmitted through a legal instrument, such as a will or trust" (AFP, 2009). While there are many books and resources "out there," and even likely on the shelves at your library about this topic, this chapter focuses upon how your organization can be successful documenting simple estate gifts with individual donors and how these donors (and in turn their dollars) can make a substantial impact for your library. Most of these steps are basic and not heavily resource (people or dollars) dependent to employ. Why? Because it is these basics that can sometimes be overlooked when discussing planned gifts. For most people—development officers included—mentioning the term "planned giving" can cause that glazed-over look (similar to discussing the finer points of physics with six-year-olds or cataloging rules with a public services colleague).

First caveat: I am not a planned giving officer who focuses on libraries; for the majority of my fundraising career, I have been a donor-centric library fundraiser who has raised significant dollars from planned gifts. I am not an attorney, CPA, or tax advisor, and any/all of the advice outlined is neither a legal nor a financial opinion. As I have worked with university libraries, I have had the opportunity to partner with talented colleagues in our gift planning offices for assistance with more complicated giving vehicles. Therein lies the difference: If I can do this, so can you.

This chapter is not highly technical about planned giving vehicles like CRATs (charitable remainder annuity trusts), CRUTs (charitable remainder unitrusts), variable gift annuities, or the like. For more about those vehicles, visit the websites of the Association of Fundraising Professionals (www.afp.org) and Partners for Philanthropic Planning (www.pppnet.org), or read Debra Ashton's *The Complete Guide to Planned Giving*, 3rd edition; or *Legacies for Libraries* by Amy Sherman Smith and Matthew D. Lehrer. There are many great resources out there if you desire more comprehensive knowledge about these topics. This chapter focuses upon key strategies that development officers, university librarians, and heads of special collections can utilize to benefit their libraries—often in short order and in a life-long relationship context.

These are ideas and best practices that I have personally learned and employed, and I am grateful for the opportunities that I have had to work with so many donors and colleagues throughout my career in development and libraries. Personally, I would encourage you to learn as much as you can from your network in library development. If you are new to the field, or are looking to expand in it, I cannot recommend more highly the Academic Library Advancement and Development Network (ALADN). Additionally, reach out to those libraries that you think "get it." Especially with planned giving, many will be happy to have you learn about their successes.

You may be reading this chapter and thinking, "But for these gifts to come in someone has to die." (I have had library colleagues in the past say those very words to me.) Yes, that is correct; they do, and we will too. You are not wishing anyone any harm by discussing their estate plans. In fact, you are actually ensuring that their legacy comes to fruition. Most older individuals are well aware of their mortality and are willing to discuss their plans with trusted friends, advisors, and colleagues. Consequently, I am not suggesting that you personally ask each and every library patron and/or colleague during your next conversation if your library is in his or her estate plan. These conversations will happen in due time.

SIMPLE BEQUESTS

What is a simple bequest? Technically, a simple bequest is a gift of personal property made through a will or trust. According to *Philanthropy Journal*, 80 percent of all charitable planned gifts come from simple bequests (Weiner, 2010). If that holds true for your library, then you are off to a great start! For purposes of this chapter, a simple estate gift is one in which a donor names your library as beneficiary of specific assets. Your library receives this gift upon the donor's death. In many cases, these planned gifts can be sizable and have a long-term impact for your organization. There are urban myths about library professionals receiving calls out of the blue from attorneys near and far sharing news of a previously unknown donor's largess. Based upon my personal experience and those of my library development colleagues, these are not urban myths—these gifts do indeed happen. I have received calls sharing a $250,000 gift from an alumni spouse who had never given us a cash gift and a $10,000 gift due to the sudden passing of a recent graduate. And while they are wonderful, they are also poignant, as we often did not interact with the donor in their lifetime, know their reasons for supporting the library, or understand what specifically they would like their funds used to support.

Where to Start

So how do you do this? First, let's find out who may already have your organization as a beneficiary in their estate plans! Yes, literally. A number of your library supporters may have already named your library as a beneficiary to their assets or a portion of their assets without your knowledge (just like the "urban myth" examples). Obtaining this information does not need to be challenging—just ask for it as you would usually ask for annual gifts and other information updates. Personally, I have seen this work exceptionally well. I know of a number of donors who chose to share this information with our library, donors whom we would have never suspected as having this type of charitable intent.

Does your library advertise the ability to make a planned gift to it? Do you have information about how to name your library as beneficiary available online? At your service desks? In your information kiosks? A number of libraries have robust planned giving programs. Congratulations if yours is one of them. I would welcome hearing your success stories. For those of you still in the beginning stages, we all started somewhere—try the above suggestions and expand through communication methods that work in your community.

For public libraries, have you sent a letter to local attorneys updating your estate language? Please do not think this is morbid! You are providing a service to your patrons—just as you are with respect to tax forms, book clubs, and other consumer information. You are informing them that just like their annual gift to your library, or their capital gift for your new building campaign, they can support the library after they leave this earth. And to be honest, libraries are late to this planned giving "game"—from hospices to health charities, art organizations to universities, this beneficiary information is often available. Without your library's information being available, a donor may not know that they can support your organization in such a way *unless you tell them*. I will never forget learning as a young development officer that the largest deterrent to giving for people was that they were never asked. And a quotation attributed to hockey great Wayne Gretzky applies in this situation: "You always miss 100 percent of the shots you don't take." Take the shot: Advertise that your library would benefit from planned gifts, supply the language, ask people to tell you their plans, and see what happens. This may seem like a very passive first approach, but it is an excellent way to get started. Also, you may have a fully developed planned giving program, but when is the last time that you sent out update letters to local attorneys? Or invited them to host a professional association meeting in your library? Or shared some of the wonderful legal history documents in your special collections area?

For those of you in situations in which you are unsure about the particular bequest language that should be used: *ask!* At colleges or universities, contact your planned giving/gift planning colleague. If you are unsure who that might be, contact your vice president of university advancement/development. And then ask the following question: Could you please supply the beneficiary designation for my library that I may use with donors who wish to leave us in their wills? This may open the floodgates, but you are looking for a simple sentence or two that they should have readily available. It will often include the formal name of the institution, your library, and possibly its location. For those of you working in public libraries, you may wish to contact your library's foundation administrator or the city/county attorney's office.

Once you have the language, you have all you need to get started. Print out some flyers, create a web link, and have the language at a service desk or two. Most libraries already have a donor (or several) who has made such a bequest. Use this as an opportunity to tell that donor's story. Create a stewardship opportunity with this donor and ask them to be your poster donor. Remember—do something with the language you receive. If you acquire a book but never catalog it, no one can find it; the same principle applies here. Burying the e-mail reply in your inbox or losing the memo with this gift language loses cash for your library.

A few paragraphs ago, I mentioned that you could reach out to area attorneys mentioning your updated language—yes, it is updated if you never supplied it before. And similarly, it is updated to your current donors, Friends group, board members, and staff if you have never shared it with them. Include it in your current mail appeal. Have a check box on your regular gift envelopes (I would like more information about leaving ABC Library in my estate plan/I have included ABC Library in my estate plan). Have a story in your newsletter. Some people will be pleased to share their plans with you. And you truly may be surprised who they are.

Beneficiaries Matter

If this idea of asking for documentation is still unsettling to you, think about it as a public service. When did you last review your own estate plans? Everyone should review their estate plans and beneficiary information annually. The prevailing thought was always to review at major life events—yet we often don't know when those might be. So reviewing annually at tax time might be a great habit to get into for you and those that your library is closest to. If you are one of the people saying "What will?" you are not alone. I cannot begin to tell you how many people do not have even simple wills. According to *Forbes*, this number hovers north of 50 percent (Ebeling, 2010). Even if you are ___ (fill in the blank with any age you like), you need a will. Put it on your to-do list for this year, or better yet, this month.

In fact, there is even a public awareness campaign called Leave a Legacy (www.leavealegacy.org) that provides information and assistance for those needing to create and update estate plans (and who plan to include charitable organizations). You may wish to see if your community has a Leave a Legacy or similar organization.

It is also important to note that naming someone as a beneficiary in your will *does not* change your beneficiaries for life insurance or retirement assets. These must be changed independently. And yes, I have heard the sad circumstances of ex-spouses receiving life insurance, a youngest child being left out of a retirement distribution, and other tales of woe. It is critical to review these documents on a periodic basis as well. Having a plan allows you (and those who care about your library) to control how they will support it after you have passed on. Without it, your legacy will not be your legacy at all.

BEQUESTS 2.0

Let's take this discussion to the next level. Three wonderful (and hypothetical) people have told you that your library is in their estate plans by contacting you after your estate update campaign. That's just great—so now what?

In an ideal world, these individuals will be happy to share ideas and copies of their plans with you. So in one you read of a specific bequest of $10,000, in another you read of a bequest of 10 percent of their estate, and in another you read that your library will receive the "rest and remainder" of their estate. Which is worth more, you ask? In all seriousness, you may not know. These are the three main types of estate gifts: a specific amount, a specific percentage of the estate, or the rest and remainder of assets once specific amounts and/or percentages are accounted for. Even if these individuals share their plans, you cannot take this money to the bank—estate plans like those mentioned in this chapter are revocable; people can change their minds (and sometimes do) about whom they wish to leave a legacy with.

Our Library Is in Their Plan—Now What?

This brings up one of the key directives/best practices of this chapter: Steward and thank them like this is a pledge without a due date! Continue to keep them engaged in the plans and ideas that made them wish to support ABC Library in the first place. How? Ask them! Consider them a new friend you need to get to know, and then build a relationship. Find out what they wish their gifts to be used for and make sure their documents clearly denote that (see below). If they like children's programming, invite them to story hour or the teen scene. If the reference section makes their heart beat faster (and actually provided them with key information about heart disease), invite them to be "guest" reference librarian of the day. These individuals are already passionate about what your library is doing, so be a great librarian and find out why! If you are struggling for new stewardship ideas, you may wish to contact or review sources provided by the Association of Donor Relations Professionals (www.adrp.net), a group of stewardship practitioners.

Just Right

We all know the children's story "Goldilocks and the Three Bears." Its principles—one was too small, one was too big, and one was just right—certainly apply to planned giving as well. We do not want individuals to be so specific with their bequests that they are almost impossible to spend; we all know stories of libraries receiving such bequests. Simply ask your library acquisitions folks about the most restrictive gift funds that they may have. Likewise, while completely unrestricted funds are fabulous, at large universities, donors *think* that since they have always supported the library, they do not need to explicitly state that in their wills. (They do!) So find a happy medium and feel free to suggest using preference criteria to donors. (Preference criteria are exactly that. For example, "I prefer my funds be used for acquisitions in Special Collections; if that is not practical, please use the funds for general acquisitions; if that is not practical, please use the funds for general library operations.") We certainly know that library materials have changed over time. Imagine the poor library that has funds restricted to spoken-word recordings (there is such a place). This is one of the key reasons why having a relationship with individual donors makes sense and why showcasing estate gifts helps you and your library plan better for the future. Have bad examples at the ready; donors aren't often aware how limiting (or how broad) their language can be.

It's Spendable, Right?

When working with planned giving donors, it is important to realize that these gifts are *not* often spendable immediately. People can change their minds (shocking, I know). The stock market may crash! This might be difficult to explain to your board or your staff. That said, if handled correctly, these dollars will be spendable for your library—maybe not by you or even your immediate successor. Even after your library is notified by an executor indicating that your library was named in a deceased benefactor's estate plan, it may take months, and even years, for your library to receive funds. Do not count on these dollars prematurely.

And even once you receive funds, they may not be spendable. Some donors will want to set up an endowment. An endowment is "a permanently restricted net asset, the principal of which is protected and the income from which may be spent and is controlled by either the donor's restrictions or the organization's governing board" (AFP, 2003: 45). Endowments may provide funds for your library permanently if invested correctly. That said, you may receive only portions of the interest as payments (you will likely not be permitted to invade the principal of the endowment). Non-endowment funds are usually considered expendable. Once they are expended (spent), they are gone.

Something else I would be remiss not to mention: Donors almost always think that the size of their bequest is "small." I have had million-dollar donors think their bequest was small, and the same with $10,000 donors. But regardless of actual size, this gift is significant to them, and you should treat it as significant to your library. You shouldn't just plan to highlight the biggest gifts in your library's publications; highlight them all. Any bequest is just the right size!

Another potential option for you to carefully consider is asking the donor who has indicated a specific priority in their estate plan (for example, monies for public programming) if they would consider making an annual contribution to begin funding their project during their lifetime. Many donors are excited to see their vision become a reality. This can often lead to that bequest remaining in the will, or potentially being tweaked in some way to better benefit the library. Most important—do not get greedy! While you may ask a donor to consider this option, be cautious!

The Best of Unshared Intentions

What do I do if they won't share their plans with me? Believe me, it happens. Some people are private. They do not want you (or anyone else) to know their plans in advance. As a colleague of mine says, "It is their money." And it is. We want them to document their plans with us so that we can be sure that the plans are clear and that we will be able to carry them out efficiently and effectively. Your library may be placed in the awkward and unfortunate situation of refusing a bequest. No library director wishes to have that happen. Additionally, you do not want to hound someone to provide the paperwork to you; it could actually make the library seem greedy or unseemly. It is a balancing act. Yet, in those cases, the best thing you can do is to continue to reach out to the individuals passively (through your library's newsletter or other vehicle) about estate planning and continue to steward them as if the money is coming sometime soon. Some elderly women especially think that if they share their plans with you, you will stop visiting or calling them, so they would rather keep you engaged without signing a gift agreement—which is okay. For every one of these potential donors, there are ten who are happy to discuss their plans and want to make sure that they are "doable." Many people are open to your suggestions once you have built a level of trust with them.

One of my own personal favorite donors—I will call her Robin—was a planned giving donor. I had the pleasure of working with her for my entire career at my current institution. She was a part of the college. Her father was on the faculty, and she retired back to town after a career in the big city. She never married; yet she loved wedding announcements. She had a zest for life and truly loved new restaurants and surprises; yet she never drove. And while she documented some of her plans, it wasn't until she passed away last year that she became the library's largest benefactor. It was her final surprise. All along, though, we treated Robin as someone who mattered to our library and its future. I could go on and on about Robin or the myriad of other donors with whom I have discussed what has yielded tens of millions of dollars in estate gifts to the libraries for which I have worked. It is important to realize that some people just wish to keep their plans private no matter how close your relationship or how wonderful your library may be.

"SPECIAL" COLLECTIONS

Potential donors may have some creative ideas about their gifts of collections—this certainly is not a surprise to many special collections or library development professionals. While the collection might be priceless to them, it may or may not meet the collecting mission of your library. *Stick with your collecting mission—or consider the serious and long-term ramifications of such a gift to your library.* It is also in good form to possibly help these potential donors find an appropriate home for their collection if it is not a good fit for your library. When you help a donor locate an institution where the collection fits the collecting needs and mission, this best serves everyone.

Over my career, I have been asked if we could keep someone's library intact and create a room for it (No), accept a collection of textiles unrelated to our mission (No), and accept numerous other collections that to the donors were priceless, but were not appropriate for our library (No). Yet I am truly happy that we were able to have those conversations prior to the phone call from an executor about a previously unknown collection for which our library was named as beneficiary. It is shocking to many people that libraries often do not want print book collections in total.

Similarly, it is very important for collections that your library does indeed want and that have been discussed with donors who wish to leave these collections in their estate plans that these plans are clearly delineated within the estate documents and that the items themselves are clearly marked in the home. Sometimes well-meaning family members are truly surprised that family letters, photographs, and/or book collections have been cataloged and promised. Sadly, I have seen promised artifacts unfortunately disappear because they were not adequately labeled. This is another reason why close relationships with local estate attorneys can only benefit your library and the needs and final wishes of the donors with whom you work.

MAINTAIN A LIST OF POTENTIAL DONORS
FOR PLANNED GIVING

Another important best practice for your library with respect to planned gifts is to keep a running list of potential donors. This list can be as simple as an Excel spreadsheet with name and inquiry date. It can be as complex as denotation in

the donor database with in-depth discussions about estate plans and even copies of the relevant documents. Make sure that your library has a copy of this
list—this is incredibly important in larger organizations like colleges and universities. Sometimes when a staff member leaves or retires, this bit of history
and donor contact gets lost, and consequently a donor's key relationship walks
away too. I have watched this happen once or twice in my career, and it is a
sad occurrence—and one that is preventable. In one such case, the university's
planned giving office was aware of the donor's intention—even though he
refused visits—but the new library administrative and development team had
no knowledge that such a potential donor existed, and a golden stewardship
opportunity was unfortunately lost.

NEXT STEPS

If you have already completed all of the steps above (did you review your
own estate plans?) and want to do more, seek out achievable action items.
Continue to look for ways to infuse gift planning into your library's overall
development program. Go back to your list of your library's top donors and
check that they have indicated whether the library is in their estate plans. If
your answer is "I am not sure" for 50 percent or more of your top 100 people,
you have a lot of work to do. This should keep you busy for some time. You
may never achieve 100 percent, but remember that the more you know, the
more you can plan for.

It would not be in the best interest of your library (or for your career) for
you to randomly pick up the phone and ask every third person on your top
100 list whether they have put the library in their estate plan: *this needs to
be part of the overall donor strategy.* Many wonderful supporters choose not
to put charities in their estate plans; remember, *it is their money.* Yet in the
context of overall gift conversations and with people whom you have built a
certain level of rapport with, you should not shrink from asking if they have
included your organization in their estate plans. They may say yes, or they
may say no, or they may say they haven't thought about it or even that they
don't have an estate plan (remember those 50 percent of people who do not).
You know what to do with the yes camp—steward them like their gifts have
already arrived. For those who say no, thank them for their continued support
of your library and say that you only asked because they have been such a
presence at your library, you had hoped they would leave a legacy. Then do
nothing other than what you would normally do: Continue to thank them for
their ongoing support. Do not apologize. Do not appear disappointed. Do not

revisit the issue (unless they do). Treat them normally and move on to the next name on your list.

For those who indicate that they haven't thought about it or don't have an estate plan, you also know what to do. You can tell both groups about the long-term needs of your library and give examples of programs and initiatives that their legacy gifts could assist with. Emphasize that every gift is significant, and provide them with the beneficiary information for your library. If they state that they do not know where to start when writing a will or developing an estate plan, you can refer them to a Leave a Legacy organization or a local community foundation. For each interaction like this, you have taken a shot—and moved closer to having additional planned giving donors in your library.

Another potential option for your library is to create a donor society for those individuals who have named your library as a beneficiary of their estate. Many larger organizations, such as colleges and universities, have such a donor recognition club. Even if you only have identified five individuals who have named your library in their plans, this could become a wonderful stewardship and engagement opportunity. First and foremost, you need to inquire if they wish to remain anonymous; some planned giving donors may want to maintain their privacy, either regarding the amount of their bequest or even regarding the existence of their plan. Over the years, I have watched such a donor society grow and flourish—individuals are often pleased to learn that their friends have included the library in their plans as well. Another caution about creating such a donor recognition club: Once you begin, you will need to continue; this type of recognition society can be time and resource intensive and should be started *after* you have begun your efforts to document existing planned gifts for your library.

SUMMARY

Over the course of this chapter, a number of basics and best practices were outlined for you concerning simple bequests that should be easily implemented for your library. First, determine what the beneficiary language is for your library. Then publicize it with your existing donors, local attorneys, your board, your staff, and your patrons. Provide people with a mechanism to document their plans with your library. Once they do so, follow up with them. Treat them like you have received their dollars already, even if they choose not to document their plans. Find out what specifically interests them about your library, and keep them engaged with it. Also, do not be afraid to consult experts. In fact, if someone mentions a gift beyond a simple bequest, do not hesitate to call in an expert.

Further, make sure that your library's needs concerning gifts in-kind are clearly articulated. Try and prevent "surprise" collections gracing your doors. Better to help donors find an alternate home for a collection sooner rather than later. Keep a running list of planned giving donors, and make sure that this list gets transitioned when staff retire or leave your organization. If you have accomplished all of these tasks, consider reaching out to all of your top 100 donors and learning if your library is included in their estate plans. Lastly, consider creating a recognition society for your planned giving donors.

If there is one piece of advice that I could leave you with, it is that bequest gifts are not scary, icky, or difficult. They are wonderful ways for special friends to support your library and the excellent work that it does. So begin your bequest quest now and see your library's dollars multiply!

REFERENCES

Ashton, Debra. 2004. *The Complete Guide to Planned Giving*. 3rd ed. Boston, MA: Jeffrey Lant and Associates.

AFP (Association of Fundraising Professionals). 2003. "Definition of Endowment." *The AFP Fund Raising Dictionary On-line*. www.afpnet.org/files/Content Documents/AFP_Dictionary_A-Z_final_6-9-03.pdf.

AFP (Association of Fundraising Professionals). 2009. "Planned-Giving Programs & the Small Nonprofit: Getting Started—Part Four." *Advancing Philanthropy*. www.afpnet.org/Publications/ArticleDetail.cfm?ItemNumber=912.

Ebeling, Ashlea. 2010. "Americans Lack Basic Estate Plans." *Forbes*. www.forbes .com/2010/03/01/estate-tax-living-will-schiavo-personal-finance-no-estate-plans .html.

Smith, Amy Sherman, and Metthew D. Lehrer. 2000. *Legacies for Libraries*. Chicago, IL: American Library Association.

Weiner, Patrick. 2010. "Talking with Donors about Bequests." *Philanthropy Journal*. www.philanthropyjournal.org/resources/fundraisinggiving/talking-with-donors -about-bequests.

10

Special Collections and Outreach

SIDNEY BERGER

Phillips Library, Peabody Essex Museum

Fundraising does not necessarily raise funds. That is why the activity is often called "development." Libraries run on resources of various kinds, and rare book and special collections departments are notorious for being expensive. Though their operations are usually figured into a parent institution's budget as a line item, booksellers will always tempt them to exceed this "guaranteed" amount, and they can usually demonstrate a need for resources beyond the budgeted amount by showing how they could use an extra cataloger or reference librarian, or how they could add significant items to the collection if the resources were sufficient.

Rare book departments are notorious black holes. No matter how much money is available to them, they can always spend more because an active collection will have gaps that booksellers will continually offer to fill, and there will almost always be backlogs of materials to catalog, with a staff too small to handle it all. There is no shortage of rare books, manuscripts, photographs, and other special collections materials available for purchase or already in hand and needing processing. Also, eventually space will become an issue—another great expense. Special collections can be money pits, especially in staffing, space, and acquisitions.

A key issue here is the last of these: adding research materials to the collections. There are many ways to accomplish this, but my focus will be on one of the paths: raising awareness of an institution's holdings within an appropriate community of potential donors. "Raising awareness" means letting people know you are there. One of the development terms for this strategy is "outreach," which itself can take many forms.

OUTREACH AS FUNDRAISING:
ENCOURAGING USE OF THE DEPARTMENT

Those in special collections may have a reputation that they oversee an exclusive department, allowing in only the upper crust of scholars and turning away anyone without "the proper credentials." This is an old-fashioned view, and it should be jettisoned, especially in an age when people are turning more and more to digital resources. To justify their existence, rare book departments should be encouraging more and more use of the original materials and rare and valuable books and manuscripts, photographs, diaries, genealogical materials, and many other things that are housed in their departments. The more physical use these departments get, the more they justify their existence, and the more they can warrant asking for sustained or increasing resources.

To increase use, the department must increase knowledge beyond its walls of what it has in its collection, what services it offers, who may use the department, and so forth. This last—who may use the department—should be just about anyone. So reaching out to a wide constituency is important. The point here is that we in the profession owe it to scholars and researchers of all kinds, of most ages, to allow access to the information we have stored up on our shelves. And we must let all potential users know what we have. This is where outreach comes in.

I say "outreach" rather than "fundraising" since this latter term does not reflect exactly what I am talking about. Outreach can take many forms. A few of them are discussed below. But first, it must be said that this endeavor takes a particular kind of person, one willing to go public about things, able to meet people, and eager to share the excitement he or she feels about the department's holdings that others might profit from. Sometimes outreach means meeting lots of people, or a few, or one. Sometimes it means being articulate about what you have and looking for innovative ways to share with others what you know. This should not be an occasional thing. The librarian should always have at the edge of her consciousness the notion that everything she does in her day as a rare book person is possibly worth sharing with others. The more people who know what your department is up to, what it has, and how it wants to invite users in, the more use the department will get. This is a desirable outcome of outreach.

This is an important point: Reaching out to many constituents is a two-way proposition. Those reached out to will benefit from the contacts they make with the library, and the department ultimately reaches out ostensibly to help others but with a clear self-interest. If the outreach makes people happy, satisfies their research needs, edifies them, and makes them indebted to the department, they are likely to offer support in cash or kind. It is not crass (it is simply a fact) to state that libraries run on donations of money and library materials, and a happy patron is more likely to support the collection than is a disgruntled one.

OUTREACH TACTICS AND BEST PRACTICES

Outreach can take many forms. Reaching out to various constituencies may be specifically to raise funds, but more often it is to raise awareness of the department. In so doing, and almost as an afterthought, the librarian may be raising the audience's awareness of the department's needs. The event or tactic need not be a specific fundraiser, but the results could be actually raising fiscal support. Or events could generate an infusion of goods or goodwill.

Outreach through Lectures

One form of outreach is a program of lectures; these should be held in one's department or in a venue close to it, if possible. No matter where the talks are given, it should be clear to the audience that the sponsoring agency is the special collections department. Lectures can be on topics drawn from the department's collections, or they could be on any of the various topics concerned with books—topics that can appeal to a wide audience: book collecting, book appraisal, book illustration, children's books, and so on. These topics can bring in a sizeable audience, and if these talks are good enough, they can engender a call for a regular series of such activities. People who frequent these events may feel like supporting the department, and such support can be solicited with fundraising brochures or other kinds of handouts to the attendees.

Outreach through Public Events

Similar to lectures, other kinds of special events in (or sponsored by) the department can be fun. These could be a book sale; a celebration of an important department milestone (an anniversary of some kind, the acquisition of a major item, the hiring of a new librarian, or some other such notable achievement); reaching a fundraising goal; a poetry reading; the visit of an author whom the department collects; or anything else that might draw a crowd. Light refreshments and signings will bring people in. The department becomes a "happening" place and will garner the goodwill of a growing clientele.

Outreach by Engaging External Organizations

Further, the librarian should be engaged with local civic organizations like the Rotary Club, Kiwanis, or fraternal groups, offering to speak to them about the library, its holdings, its special collections, or anything else that might be of use to them. One lecture I gave to a group was on how to store and conserve their own personal collections. Another was on archiving their family papers and photographs and cataloging their own book collections. Workshops on these topics, or on collecting ephemera, or on doing simple bookbinding, can draw people interested in books and can be excellent outreach opportunities.

Outreach through Exhibits

Special collections departments often have exhibition or display space. People like seeing attractive exhibits. These departments should have an exhibit space with changing content, partly for preservation reasons, and partly to bring in people who wish to see the new materials on display. They should, of course, mount shows that draw from the department's treasures. And the librarians should make these shows known to the public in any way they can. One means is through social networking (more on this later); another is by creating a checklist or catalog for the exhibit, if funding for it is available. A simple checklist is easy. Each item in the display will presumably have a label. A simple listing of the labels is enough to create the checklist. These can be handed out for free to anyone seeing the exhibit.

Outreach through Publications

This is a good segue to publications, perhaps the most lasting and most impactful of outreach efforts. Newsletters, pamphlets, exhibit catalogs, and news releases are among the many regular or occasional publications that are useful for reaching potential donors. Maintaining a mailing list of potential donors and others who might be interested in what the department wishes to make known—recent acquisitions, milestones of the collection or the librarians, publications of the staff, discoveries in the stacks, highlighted important holdings, upcoming lectures or workshops, and so forth—is important.

If an exhibit catalog is produced, the librarian should consider offering it to the Rare Books and Manuscripts Section (RBMS) Exhibition Awards Committee for one of its annual awards (RBMS, 2014). The Committee accepts catalogs of all kinds, analog and digital, at all price levels. After the submissions have been judged and the winners announced (at the annual RBMS preconference), all submissions go on display, and a list of them is published online, often with a paper brochure. Even for those which did not win an award, the publicity can be beneficial.

The department may have important unpublished materials: manuscripts, collections of correspondence, drawings or sketches, or ephemera of various kinds. An enterprising librarian might create a publication about such collections. I have always advised my staff that publications are excellent for their own careers, and the publications highlight the collections the staff work in and bring honor to the institution. All rare book staff should always be thinking about ways to bring the collection's holdings before an audience, scholarly or not. And materials from the department's collection are obvious sources of information for such publications. A successful publication, handsomely produced, can also bring financial rewards for the institution.

One good example of such a publication is a modest pamphlet put out by the Houghton Library at Harvard University, *Marbled and Paste Papers: Rosamond Loring's Recipe Book* (Cambridge, MA: Houghton Library, Harvard College Library, 2007). The pamphlet's editor, Hope Mayo, recognized the importance of the manuscript notebook, knew there would be an audience for it, edited it, transcribed it, commissioned an introductory article for it, and published it as a small monograph. The importance of this text was not lost on its audience: the pamphlet sold well. Such publications do not need to be expensively produced, and they can be superb tools for outreach for the department. Also, many special collections departments create small brochures—sometimes nothing more than a trifold sheet—highlighting individual collections. Certainly, this information can be disseminated online, but it is a good advertising practice for the department to be able to send out such brochures in the mail to prospective scholars and to hand them out to visitors.

Librarians will usually want to keep their departments before the eyes of as many people as they can. For this reason, one form of outreach that may garner great benefit is news releases—another form of publication. When the librarian discovers an amazing item on the shelves, when a lecture or workshop is forthcoming, when an important acquisition is made or a milestone is reached, it takes little time to send out a news release on it. A well-written press release can pique the interest of a reporter at a newspaper or at a TV or radio station, and this can lead to an article in a local paper or a slot on the evening news. Such publicity can bring in many potential donors since it is likely to get out to a much greater audience than the librarian could have reached on his own. Libraries love milestones: the rare book department is celebrating its twenty-fifth anniversary; the special collections department has just acquired its four hundred thousandth volume (or its millionth manuscript); the department has just acquired the one volume for which it has been searching for thirty years; the rare book department has just mounted its one hundredth exhibit; and so forth. Many things can generate provocative news releases.

It should be added, however, that most institutions have marketing departments, which do not want individual parties outside their department reaching out to the public without the institution's stamp of approval. So the special collections librarian should work closely with marketing to develop a strategy and a plan of action for announcing the department's finds and events, milestones, and publications.

Outreach to Booksellers

Reaching out through press releases gets information out to large audiences. On a much narrower, more focused level, the librarian can reach out to individual people: dealers, collectors, donors, public figures, or anyone else who might profit from knowing about the department's collections and who might someday be in a position to help the department. Particular dealers and collectors are serious candidates for such outreach since, if they are chosen correctly, they will be specialists in the areas of collecting that the department is strong in. Dealers can be befriended, and then they may feel a sense of kinship with the department, so they may give the department right of first refusal of important materials they acquire. I have had dealers offer my library great things before offering them to anyone else. And departments I have worked in have also been the recipients of gifts from dealers whose generosity and kindness link the department closely to them. There is a symbiosis: dealers need the departments to sell things to; the departments need the dealers to find the items they need for their collections. So befriending dealers—getting to know the dealers who specialize in the things your department collects—is a good form of outreach. Everyone profits. Not to mention that dealers are often wonderful people who may become your friends and friends of your institution, not just your business acquaintances.

Since the outreach should be to anyone who might profit from the department or whom the department can profit from, reaching out in various ways to booksellers can reap rewards for your department. As I have said, these dealers can be your best allies in helping you to build your collections. The outreach can take the form of lunches (that you or your department pays for—do not let the dealer treat you, as it can be seen as a conflict of interest), notices to the dealers of items you have in your collection, want lists, requests for information, and so forth. Some of your best contacts—your most loyal allies—can be booksellers. RBMS has created a document on ethical standards in which is discussed the taking of gifts and other dispensations from booksellers. Meals are on the list, but this is not a hard-and-fast prohibition. The document is worth consulting with care (RBMS, 2003).

Outreach to Collectors

Similarly, getting to know those who collect in areas of your department's strengths can allow you to forge strong friendships that can lead to donations. Some of the great institutional collections were begun by private parties whose passion and insight, enthusiasm, and resources were devoted to amassing important holdings in clearly defined subjects. Often private collections become part of an institution's holdings. Using whatever resources the librarian has at her disposal, she should try to locate appropriate collectors and get to know them. An old tactic that has been successful is to offer to put on an exhibition at the institution of selections from the library of a private collector. It may come across as flattery, but a department that has strong holdings in that person's area could offer a joint exhibition, showing the public superb items from the two collections. Doing a catalog for this exhibit can endear this person even more to the institution. One result is the placement (for as long as the exhibit is on) of the collector's goods in the institution's hands. Such a "picture" could suggest an appropriate final home for the collector's books and manuscripts. He will see that the host institution will care for and properly display the items he has spent a good portion of his life and resources to amass. As a part of fundraising efforts, librarians should work with potential donors of collections to also leave funds to cover the cost of processing and upkeep of their collection.

Outreach to Authors

Another group to reach out to is authors, whose papers and books may well grace your special collections department. The standard tack to take with an author is something like this: "You have built up an important collection of papers and books. You are mortal. You need to make plans for these. We are here to help you. We can guarantee your immortality in these items. We will put them into a safe storage facility. We will catalog your books and manuscripts. We will honor your requests as to the availability of these materials to scholars." And so forth. Also, you would like the authors to sign over the rights to your institution, if they are willing to do so. One thing to tell authors is that if they leave the rights to others, at some time in the future those rights might be abused or misused. By giving the rights to an institution and specifying how they are to be controlled, the author can guarantee to perpetuity that these rights will be properly handled.

Much more could be said about outreach to authors, especially with respect to the legal and access issues concerning their manuscripts. But the main point here is that authors' papers are some of the most precious collections that rare book libraries have, and such libraries can show authors why they are excellent repositories for these materials. One librarian in the Midwest has reached out to a host of science fiction writers and has brought in a superb collection of manuscripts. This kind of outreach, done with the enthusiasm of the serious collector or dedicated rare book librarian, can yield excellent results for the department.

Outreach to Businesses or Local Organizations

A keen special collections librarian can also reach out to local businesses or organizations, offering to help them organize and place their archives. This can generate much goodwill, and it can result in the department's acquiring important local civic or business records. Such acquisitions may be accompanied by funding to do the processing and cataloging, and the relationship that is established between the department and the other entity could lead to long-term cooperation in activities and possibly support for the department.

Outreach through a Book Collection Contest

Engaging people in the world of rare books, especially in such a way that it calls attention to the special collections department, is a good form of outreach. One means of doing this is to sponsor a book collecting contest for students. This will take some planning, but these contests are engaging, fun, and educational, and they can generate good publicity. They take sponsors, perhaps local booksellers or businesses, perhaps dedicated faculty of the institution. Best is to get the prizes endowed so that a fund for cash prizes will be available each year. Awards at different levels or for different categories can be given (e.g., prizes can be given for collections of fiction and nonfiction, for ephemera, for particular subject areas, and for undergraduate and graduate students). Local bookstores may offer gift cards as prizes. Award ceremonies may be covered by the press, and they could include dinners or breakfasts. A good press release announcing the contest (perhaps with flyers posted around the institution) will get the word out to school and other local media outlets. Similarly, winners can be written up for the same media. And rare book departments are the logical sponsoring agency for such contests, so they can get good press for the entire project.

Outreach through a Website and through Social Media

Another form of outreach, though it is not often thought of as such, is a good website. When anyone wants to know about your department, she is likely to turn to the Internet. The library should be prominently displayed on the institution's home page. That is, a searcher should not have to click beyond the institution's home page to find a link to the library. And the special collections department should be only a single click away from the library's home page. This might take some politicking to effect such prominence on a website, but it is well worth the effort.

The site for the department should be simple and clear, easy to read and navigate, and filled with information that any searcher might want: who you are; where you are; your hours; your holdings—strengths and special collections; your staff (with contact points); your use policies and procedures; and so forth. The site should be congenial, with good graphics and a friendly and welcoming attitude, and showing a willingness to help all who contact the department. Prominent on the department's home page should be a link to a fundraising page that allows online donations to be made to the special collections department. The site may also have a direct link to the library's online catalog and links to finding aids to the department's important collections, images of some of the library's treasures, and even biographies of its permanent personnel. And it should make it apparent that the department is eager to serve its clientele. This is outreach at its most apparent and functional.

For several years now, special collections departments have taken advantage of social media to reach out to a huge audience. Twitter, Facebook, Flickr, Pinterest, Myspace, blogs, and many other such media are like free advertising sites for the department. Wikipedia lists nearly 350 social networking websites, and more are being created daily (Wikipedia, 2013). This is a superb way to get your name and information about the department and its holdings out into the world.

One person in the department should be designated to be the keeper of social media output, but all should be encouraged to supply text. Anyone working in the department is likely to come up with some newsworthy item: a discovery in the stacks, a recent acquisition, the recognition that the department is celebrating some milestone, or anything else worth telling the world about. The single voice will keep the communiques uniform in language and tone and will prevent duplication of messages. Social media can be the ultimate tool in outreach, for a well-handled post can reach millions of people in a short time.

Outreach through Friends Groups

A feature of many rare book departments is a Friends of the Library group. In the museum world they are called Library Visiting Committees. Some people think these groups are more trouble than they are worth, but a strong literature shows that they can be tremendously useful to the department (Elder and Steele, 2000; Smith and Martin, 1994). The Friends can do many of the outreach things delineated here and spare the efforts of the staff. Membership in these groups can be limited or open, depending on who is running the group. And there can be dues of some kind that may raise resources for the department. The librarian may be directly involved, depending on the role of the Friends group, or he may play no role in the group's activities other than an advisory one. It depends on how much time the librarian has to spare and how much direction the group needs. This kind of outreach can pay big dividends, however. I know of a group that has given many thousands of dollars to the department they are Friends of, coming up with extraordinary funds for special purchases, locating important collectors who could become donors to the library, and running events that bring in crowds—events that the library staff does not have the time to put on themselves. Friends groups can be a chore and a time-sink, but they can also be some of your best advocates in the philanthropic world.

Outreach through Adopt-a-Book Programs

An activity that I have seen used successfully at a few institutions is an Adopt-a-Book or Adopt-a-Manuscript program (for purchase or conservation). The aim is to get people jazzed about the department and its holdings and allow them to help the library by sponsoring the purchase of special items or covering the cost of conservation for damaged materials. One library ran an Adopt-a-Book program by identifying about one hundred great treasures that could use conservation work. The clients bid on the items, with a minimum starting bid large enough to cover the cost of conservation. The "winners" paid for the conservation and got their names in a published volume of treasures of the library—the very treasures that were bid on. The final volume had before-and-after photos of the treated items, along with the names of the people who were enlightened and generous enough to pay for their conservation. People loved these books, and they loved helping the deeply grateful library.

One last note: Outreach means going beyond the institution. Many organizations, with their expensive branding, will want any outreach to be vetted by the appropriate department, which may bring benefits in that this department has experts in effective outreach, and they can do a better job for the special collections department than the librarians could have done on their own.

OUTREACH: A CASE HISTORY

As mentioned above, one relatively easy form of outreach is connecting with local media. The rare book librarian can conjure up press releases for any number of reasons and can look to local events outside the library as opportunities for outreach.

One tactic that I employed at the University of California, Riverside can be seen as a case study in outreach. It might not work for everyone, but it worked superbly for the library I was overseeing at the time, and in any community in which rare book fairs are a drive away, it might be practicable. Here is the story.

The University of California, Riverside has the J. Lloyd Eaton Collection of Science Fiction, Fantasy, Horror, and Utopia, the finest such collection in the galaxy, with over 100,000 monographs, more than 50,000 fantasy-type comic books, close to 100,000 issues of fanzines (the newsletters of science-fiction fan clubs), full runs of scores of science fiction (sf) periodicals, sf writers' manuscripts, hundreds of shooting scripts for sf and fantasy movies, dozens of thousands of graphic novels, and much more. The collection's early volumes go back to a 1517 edition of Thomas More's *Utopia* and seventeenth-century imaginary voyages. There are also first editions of Mary Shelley's *Frankenstein* (1818), Bram Stoker's *Dracula* (1897), H. G. Wells's *Time Machine* (1895), and the works of just about every sf writer in the twentieth century. They have one of the scarce copies of Ray Bradbury's *Fahrenheit 451* (1953) in the asbestos binding. And on and on. And the library holds works in dozens of languages.

The Antiquarian Booksellers Association of America (ABAA) holds its annual West Coast book fair alternately in Los Angeles or San Francisco. When it was in LA one year, I spoke with the fair organizers to ask if they would want to have a truly wonderful exhibit of sf books at the book fair. The genre has millions of readers, especially in southern California, where the film industry produces one sf/fantasy/horror movie after another. Further, Riverside is only about seventy-five miles from the convention center where the book fair was to be held, so it would be easy to mount an extensive showing of items in this glitzy genre.

And glitzy it is, since just about every dust jacket for the hardbound books and every cover of the paperbacks has original artwork. The thousands upon thousands of issues of sf magazines are likewise adorned with wild and wonderful, colorful and startling art. The bindings on some of the nineteenth-century volumes in this genre (especially, for instance, the Jules Verne novels) are strikingly beautiful. Even the crude fanzines have captivating drawings on them, and they also offer the first writings of budding sf authors like Ray

Bradbury and Isaac Asimov. Equally eye-catching are the covers and the internal art of the graphic novels and the Japanese anime volumes.

It was not difficult for the fair organizers to see that this could be a truly captivating exhibit, especially since there are hordes of collectors of these things all over the place, and they are interested in the kinds of things that many of the dealers at the fair would be selling. It would be good for all concerned: collectors, the booksellers, and the library, for we would be able to inform a large number of people about the Riverside Eaton Collection.

The curator of the Eaton Collection at the time was George Slusser, who was as knowledgeable as anyone about sf and its associated genres, and who was intimately familiar with the collection at UC Riverside. With his help, the special collections department selected a great number of exciting, important, showy, historically significant items. We were asked how many vitrines we wanted for the show. We said, "How many can you spare? We have enough great things to fill dozens of cases." We wound up with eighteen large glass cases, and we filled them with some of the most attention-grabbing items we could find. It was not difficult, since we had hundreds of thousands to choose from.

Ray Bradbury lived at that time in Palm Springs, in the desert beyond Riverside. We contacted him and told him of the event, and we said we would devote a large vitrine to his works. We asked if he would like to be present. He was delighted to join us. So we designed a poster to advertise the event featuring him and his books. Later on, during the fair, he was surrounded by fans, and he was asked to sign dozens of these posters. Bringing him to the fair in person gave us the opportunity to announce to the public that he would be there, no doubt increasing the number of attendees significantly.[1]

This brings up one of the tactics of outreach that I spoke of above. We were fortunate that the book fair organizers saw this exhibit, as we did, as a great drawing card. They did extensive advertising of the fair, possibly more than they normally would have, and they made a big point of the fact that UC Riverside's special collections department would be mounting a large exhibition of sf materials. They were also as elated as we were that Bradbury would be there, and that was prominently noted in their ads. I called several local newspapers (including the *Los Angeles Times*) and radio and TV stations to let them know about the event, and we sent out press releases as well. Local papers covered the fair, with an emphasis on the exhibition.

The day before the fair was to open, a Thursday, we had to convey all of our materials to the convention center. We could have used a station wagon or one of the university's little buses. But I wanted to do something much more ostentatious. I engaged Brinks, one of the oldest and best-known security transport companies in the United States. About two hours before the loaded truck took off from Riverside for the LA convention center, I called a few newspapers to let them know that we would be pulling up at the convention center loading dock at a particular time, with a Brinks-load of sf treasures. When the truck arrived, reporters and cameramen were there from the *Los Angeles Times* and other papers.

I had carefully loaded the Brinks truck so that when we opened it, we had a box of particularly showy books just inside. We opened the truck and I opened this carton and pulled out one of the gorgeous Jules Verne first editions, with a glowing red-and-gold-decorated cover. A cameraman posed us with me holding this volume, with a view of the Brinks name on the truck, and with a view, also, of the Brinks guard with his gun prominently holstered in the frame. The picture appeared in several local community papers that evening and the next morning on the front page of the *Los Angeles Times* local news section.

We had done a good job of selecting for this exhibition. There were cases devoted to great authors, to fanzines, to sf magazines, to graphic novels, to historically important works, and so forth. The exhibit was truly a splash of color and image, and it was obvious when the doors opened that something extraordinary was taking place. Usually, the first people through the door of ABAA fairs are serious collectors who aim for the booksellers they know best. This crowd had an equal number of people who made a beeline for the exhibit at the back of the hall. Later on, the fair organizers told me that the attendance at the fair was twice what they had expected, far exceeding the numbers for previous fairs. Booksellers over the next two-and-a-half days told me that they had never before had such a busy experience. The place was mobbed with people. Once they had spent their time at the exhibit—and some of them spent hours there, talking with special collections staff and Bradbury—people went to the booths, and sales were reportedly extremely good at this fair. We handed out hundreds of posters, Eaton Collection brochures, and business cards.

I was startled by the number of times people said to me, "I didn't know of your Eaton Collection," or "I have been a science fiction reader since my childhood. I have hundreds of books and never knew what to do with them." I heard that people had traveled from as far as San Francisco and Arizona to attend, solely on the basis of their interest in sf. We had created some pamphlets about the Eaton Collection and about the special collections department, and we gave them out by the handful. We took down names of people who had collections and who said they were interested in finding homes for their childhood comic books and paperbacks. (Remember, most sf books were never issued in hard covers. In most instances, paperbacks were the only manifestations of these popular, "ephemeral" books.)

The buzz generated by this exhibit before, during, and after the fair was palpable. And for months afterward, we got phone calls and letters in the mail from people offering us their collections. One person had a splendid collection of superb fantasy comic books—many thousands of them. His whole collection wound up at Riverside. The department received many gifts, and even if they contained duplicates for us, these were tradable to a dealer or to other collectors for items we did not have. The book fair operators covered most of the expenses—even the cost of the Brinks truck. So the benefits to the special collections department were great—in acquisitions, goodwill, and advertising—and the department's outlay was minimal.

Granted, this was an extraordinary opportunity that was made possible by an extraordinary collection that lent itself to just such an affair. But there are lessons to be learned here. First, rare book departments should constantly look for opportunities to link up with external events. If a medical convention is to be held, why not offer to have on display your department's most alluring medical books? Conferences on all kinds of topics are held throughout the year in the larger cities around the country. Enterprising special collections librarians should know who is coming to town and should try to use these events as forums for displaying their holdings.

One caution, of course, is that the venue must be secure and the cases should be environmentally sound. Security should be tight, with a guarantee that it will be in place round the clock through the duration of the event. Security was clearly not a problem for us at the ABAA book fair.

Another thing to be learned is that each rare book department is likely to have some special collection that is worth exhibiting, and the librarian should always be on the lookout for a place to show it. Further, good outreach to public media like newspapers and TV and radio stations can generate much free advertising. Today, with social media what they are, this kind of information can go out to literally millions of people in a short time. Departments should be plugged into Facebook and Twitter and other such networks, and they should have blogs that highlight great items or collections in their libraries. All media, electronic or on paper, should clearly state what the institution is and how to contact it. Who are the contact people? What services do they offer? What collections are their strengths? How do I donate to the collection? And so forth.

The Eaton experience did not generate a vast amount of funds. It did, however, generate many donations of books and other materials. It widened the circle of people who knew about the Riverside collection, and it brought goodwill to the department, often in the form of gifts.

One other thing worth mentioning is that the whole event was really fun to do. It gave us in the special collections department the opportunity to get out of our daily routines (not that there are really "routines" in special collections departments), to delve into one of our most exciting collections, to handle great things, to pick and choose among them, to display them, and to meet hordes of people interested in what we had and grateful for our efforts. When librarians have the chance to dig deeply into their special holdings, they will come up with many oohs and aahs, and with an appreciation for those who put these collections together in the first place and who have given us the pleasure of being caretakers of them.

To reiterate: not every department will be able to match the glitz and excitement of the Eaton experience, but the opportunities are there for approaching this level of activity. It takes a good eye, a good imagination, and a willingness to reach out to a community of people just waiting to be reached out to.

CONCLUSION

Outreach is one of the major components of development. The goal could be to raise funds, but it could just as well be to notify the world about the department, which can bring benefits of many kinds beyond the fiscal. Increased use, donations of collections, a wide understanding of the department's holdings and functions, and an increased audience to which to disseminate information should be the goals of all special collection departments—and good outreach can accomplish these.

NOTE

1. As a footnote, and not related to this chapter, but worth recording somewhere (and it might as well be here), is this anecdote, which I have been thinking about for decades and never wrote down till now. At this book fair, Ray Bradbury told me he had been invited to the White House for a major event. Each attendee entering had to sign a guest book. The person who immediately preceded him was Bill Gates. So under Gates's name, Bradbury wrote his name and the note, "I do not do Windows."

REFERENCES

Elder, Steven, and Vicki Steele. 2000. *Becoming a Fundraiser: The Principles and Practice of Library Development.* Chicago: American Library Association.
RBMS (Rare Books and Manuscripts Section). 2003. "RBMS Code of Ethics." www .rbms.info/about/#ethics.

RBMS (Rare Books and Manuscripts Section). 2014. "RBMS Exhibition Awards Committee." www.rbms.info/committees/exhibition_awards/index.shtml.

Smith, Elaine B., and Robert Martin. 1994. "Working with Friends of the Library to Augment Staff Resources: A Case History." *Rare Books & Manuscripts Librarianship* 9, no. 1:19–28. http://rbm.acrl.org/content/rbml/9/1/19.full.pdf+html.

Wikipedia. 2013. "List of Social Networking Websites." http://en.wikipedia.org/wiki/List_of_social_networking_websites.

11

A Public Library's Multifaceted Approach to Fundraising

Gina Millsap and LeAnn Meyer
Topeka and Shawnee County Public Library
and the Library Foundation

Successful fundraising programs come in all shapes and sizes, but when it comes down to the details of actually raising funds and making your big ask, fundraising initiatives should be tailored to your organization's needs and resources. Effective fundraising utilizes best practices based on the development of strong relationships with donors that require cultivation, management, and stewardship. The Topeka and Shawnee County Public Library, Friends of the Topeka and Shawnee County Public Library, and the Library Foundation (of the Topeka and Shawnee County Public Library) make up the fundraising team that identifies needs, quantifies resources, and implements the donor strategies that result in funding. We refer to these entities as a three-legged stool: three organizations that are interdependent and clear on their individual roles, and that do their part to help make a great library.

While there is a great deal of fine print on how this three-legged stool was built, let's scrap the blueprints and paint a simple picture. First, imagine trying to place a two-legged stool on the floor. A stool with just two legs soon keels over. Originally, fundraising was shared between the library and the Friends, but, like that third leg, a key component was missing. When it was determined that the library needed a new facility, a more robust approach to fundraising was deemed necessary.

In 1982, the Friends took the lead to incorporate the Library Foundation. The foundation helps secure financial resources to support library collections, programs, services, technology, and physical facilities. It cultivates and solicits philanthropic support by providing stewardship of assets entrusted to it and by encouraging appropriate community partnerships.

To expand a bit on the role of the Friends versus that of the foundation, it is important for libraries that have both affiliated organizations to ensure that their purpose, operations, and how they interact with donors is clearly articulated and distinct. In our case, the Friends raise funds through their enterprises. The Friends manage three lines of business: an annual book sale and semi-annual bag sales (think of them as wholesale outlets); their Booktique, a used-book and gift shop (a retail operation); and online sales, which is projected to provide more revenue than the book sales in the next few years.

The library's strategic plan drives requests to the foundation and the Friends. Requests, based on staff recommendations, are made formally from the library board of trustees to the Library Foundation Board or the Friends of the Library Board. The Friends take an entrepreneurial approach to make resources available for library initiatives. The foundation uses its fundraising programs to respond to funding requests and to grow assets under management (see Figure 11.1).

All three organizations operate within the framework of the library's strategic plan and adopt the library's mission statement: "Your Place. Stories you want, information you need, connections you seek."

HOW DO YOU RAISE $200,000?

Fast forward to September 26, 2013, when we find ourselves in front of a room of fifty people including library staff members and trustees, a bank president with his staff, and the media holding a larger-than-life check for $200,000. This check symbolizes years of strategic planning and relationship development. It also exemplifies rallied support of the impact our library makes in this community. Though I could list the steps we have taken to reach this moment, I still find myself asking, "How the heck did we get here?"

Need for the Project

It starts with community needs. More than 100,000 people visit our bookmobiles annually and check out 300,000 items, which is 15 percent of the library's circulation. The Topeka and Shawnee County Public Library's fundamental goal and responsibility is to ensure service equity to citizens in our community. Our challenge is to make sure that library services, collections, and programs are available on an equitable basis to the 178,000 people living in the 550-square-mile service area—with no branches. The bookmobiles play an integral role in delivering a quality library experience and represent a cost-effective and resource-efficient substitute for building and maintaining branches.

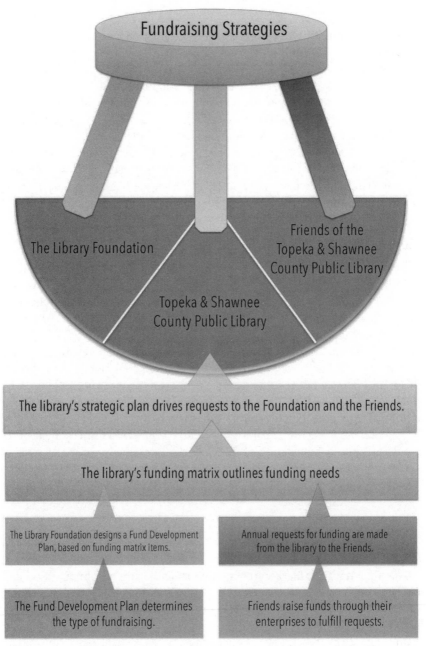

Figure 11.1.   Three-legged stool. (Credit: LeAnn Meyer, administrative specialist, the Library Foundation)

Need for Funding

The library currently owns and operates two bookmobiles, serving the general public, that are open ninety-two hours each week at eighteen locations. The well-loved and well-used bookmobiles are aging and at the end of vehicle life. The advanced age of the vehicles and their specialized nature have made it difficult to locate the necessary replacement parts to adequately repair them. Frequent interruptions in service have caused vehicles regularly to miss scheduled stops and disappoint thousands of customers.

Library management decided to proceed with a replacement plan, as the vehicles were due to retire within a few years. A process review team conducted an extensive analysis to evaluate the library's current method of using bookmobiles for its vehicle-based, community outreach services. Included in the process review was a customer survey given to current bookmobile customers, a community needs analysis, and an assessment of the cost-effectiveness of the service.

Results of the final process review indicated that bookmobiles remained the library's best method for deploying library services equitably to its customers in the library's service area. Library management concluded that new vehicle purchases would provide a life span of at least twenty years of service delivery and meet the objectives in the library's Community Services Plan.

In December 2012, the library board of trustees sent a resolution to the Library Foundation to request funding for a new bookmobile. In February 2013, the library CEO and foundation executive director, in consultation with the foundation board, decided that the fundraising strategy would be to solicit a gift and designate the donor as a "Literacy Partner."

The process to secure a major gift requires a substantial investment of resources. With the solicitation of this major gift, we knew we would need to cultivate a small number of donor prospects with significant giving capacity. We knew that going in, and we expected to speak with and make the case for support to multiple prospects. We were thrilled that one donor agreed to be the primary funder.

Literacy Partnership Strategy

It was important to find a corporate donor that shared the library's organizational values and was committed to literacy and learning. We identified a grant-making organization with a history of supporting educational community initiatives.

In April 2013, the Library Foundation invited a local bank foundation, Capitol Federal Foundation, to become a Literacy Partner with the Topeka and Shawnee County Public Library to promote reading and life-long learning to enhance the lives of all citizens in our community. The Library Foundation requested a charitable gift of $200,000 from the Capitol Federal Foundation to provide funding to purchase a new bookmobile for the community.

The first contact was through the Library Foundation's treasurer, who was the first vice president and CEO for Capitol Federal. He acted as a door opener, paving the way for the official "ask." The foundation board chair, foundation executive director, and the library CEO then followed up with a meeting with the Capitol Federal Foundation's executive director to make the ask.

In our case for support, we emphasized the emotional connection a company can make by aligning its values with the aspirational values of the library. We also noted that a partnership would raise the profile and create greater awareness of both organizations in the community. Capitol Federal Foundation agreed to become a Literacy Partner with the Topeka and Shawnee County Public Library and to provide $200,000 to fund the project.

Benefits of a Literacy Partnership

As Literacy Partners, Capitol Federal and the Topeka and Shawnee County Public Library reinforce the importance of investing in literacy and learning. Capitol Federal also recognizes the value of its name appearing daily to thousands of community members for twenty years. We intend to use this as a model for future major gift donors.

Figure 11.2 is a "conceptual illustration" of the new bookmobile, highlighting a literacy partnership between Capital Federal and the Topeka and Shawnee County Public Library. A design team, made up of marketing

CAPITOL FEDERAL®
AND TOPEKA & SHAWNEE COUNTY PUBLIC LIBRARY
LITERACY PARTNERSHIP

Conceptual Illustration*

Figure 11.2. Bookmobile conceptual illustration. (Credit: Rich Kobs, art director, Topeka and Shawnee County Public Library)

professionals from each organization, is working to produce a design for the exterior wrap for the vehicle that will be striking and attention-getting and will promote the partnership and brands of both organizations.

Working with Other Donors

So back to the room and the $200,000 check. It takes thirty seconds to ask for money; it takes much longer to build a partnership with a donor based on trust, understanding, and shared values. The time and resources utilized to reach this moment were key elements in our fundraising strategy. So was our partnership approach.

While we sought funding for the bookmobile, we also cultivated donors for our Kids Library project. As part of the library's strategic plan, the Kids Library was reimagined and reengineered as a place children and their parents could visit and return to over and over again. Our goal was to create a space that inspires imagination, learning, literacy, and fun. The transformation, which included five 3-D structures in all, was paid for by $200,000 in private donations, the approximate cost of the project.

There were several generous donors, but the Junior League of Topeka's $75,000 gift in celebration of its seventy-fifth anniversary was the lead gift and an eagerly sought partnership. The Library Foundation competed with a number of other community organizations to make the case that the Kids Library was the perfect fit for the Junior League's goal of funding a project that would have a lasting impact on children and families. This donation is a prime example of how a library's goals and a donor's philanthropic goals can align and result in a project that will make a real difference in the lives of the children and families in a community.

WHERE THE REAL MONEY IS—PLANNED GIVING

Major gifts, like the ones above, can have a lasting impact and also meet an immediate need. To meet the future needs of the library and sustain them over time, you need different fundraising strategies and more money. One of the simplest and most popular ways to make a gift that will live on after someone passes is to give through a will or trust—also known as planned giving.

"Americans will transfer at least $41 trillion between 1998–2052, according to a study by the Social Welfare Research Institute at Boston College. At least $6 trillion of that funding will be bequests to charity," according to authors Paul Schervish and John Havens, who wrote that "a golden age of philanthropy is dawning" (Henze, 2004: 1).

The library has had a planned giving program since May 1998. This is a bit unusual for a library foundation of its size, but it has turned out to be one of the most strategic and effective decisions we have made.

Planned giving may appear to be the fundraising program with the least return on investment (ROI), especially for libraries that have immediate funding needs. The industry standard is seven to ten years from time of commitment to actual receipt of funds. However, a donor's planned gift may be many times more than their largest single gift or a cumulative annual gift.

The Wilder Society

Creating some type of a recognition program for planned giving can also be a valuable tool. While some donors prefer anonymity, many people enjoy and appreciate receiving recognition for their generosity regardless if the gift is immediate or delayed.

We initiated our planned giving program by establishing the Edward and Mary Wilder Society. The Wilder Society recognizes donors who have included the Library Foundation in their estate planning through bequests, trusts, charitable gift annuities, or other similar gift arrangements. Also, the Wilder Society recognizes donors who have made planned gifts, deferred gifts, or committed annual gifts to the Library Foundation, the Friends of the Library, or the Topeka and Shawnee County Public Library.

Early benefactors Edward and Mary Wilder helped raise the funds to build the first permanent library in Topeka. The Wilders made a lifetime commitment, primarily through donations of art that has enhanced the experience of visiting and using the library to this day. This memorial gift created the first public art collection in the city.

We promote and explain membership in the Wilder Society with what we call the Four *A*s:

- Amount: The Edward and Mary Wilder Society recognizes donors who have made planned or deferred gifts to the Library Foundation, the Friends of the Library, or the Topeka and Shawnee County Public Library. There is no minimum gift amount required for membership. Any planned or deferred gift qualifies. A percentage amount is also accepted.
- Anonymous: Donors may choose to remain anonymous if they wish. We are glad to honor the request of any donor who wishes to remain anonymous.
- Annual: An annual lifetime gift that is significant for the donor also qualifies for membership. The amount specified by the donor can be contributed annually for the duration of an individual's lifetime.

- Assets: Gifts of assets such as appreciated stock, real estate, life insurance, and tangible personal property (fine art) qualify as planned gifts by virtue of their dollar value.

To engage Wilder Society members and to grow membership, an event known as the Wilder Society Tea began in 1999. It started as a modest program and has grown into a highly anticipated event meant to fire the imagination and inspire donors to make a gift that will make a difference in library services, collections, and programs for years to come.

The teas are held on Sunday afternoons and always have a theme. They are also accompanied by delicious finger food and desserts. A program of interest to the Wilder Society member demographic is provided. Note that most members belong to the Matures Generation (born before 1945)—it's important that we have food, content, and scheduling that appeals to them. Many of them prefer daytime events since driving at night is difficult.

Some examples of these themes are as follows:

- The Maltese Falcon—performance and discussion of a renowned book presented by library staff
- Japanese Tea Ceremony Tea—program included a video from the Japanese consulate office
- A Sunday Safari—world-famous former zoo director Gary Clarke telling stories
- Genealogy Tea—program on genealogy and genealogy resources available at the library

Things to Consider

Planned giving programs take time—lots of it. The Library Foundation originally had one full-time staff person dedicated to planned giving. In some ways, that was ideal, especially since, with the exception of donors who had contributed to the capital campaign during the library's construction from 1999 to 2001, there was no real donor base. While designated staff is ideal, it is not always possible with a small foundation. However, even allocating one day a week would be useful and have long-term benefits for funding library projects and for growing a foundation's assets under management.

Planned giving takes money. There needs to be an adequate budget to support the planned giving activities. It requires significant staff time devoted to the following:

- Getting to know donors and develop relationships built on trust
- Developing an understanding by the donor of the institution's goals
- Facilitating the achievement of the donor's philanthropic goals

Here's the ROI

From 1998 to 2013, the Wilder Society has grown from fewer than 100 members to more than 200 members. Over the past fifteen years, the library has received bequests and other memorial gifts totaling $2,385,701.98. Those funds will be used to fulfill the library's strategic goals and ensure continued excellence in the future.

According to Nancy Lindberg, executive director of the Library Foundation of the Topeka and Shawnee County Public Library,

> Planned giving is a special form of fundraising that can pay the most dividends as long as you have the comfort of time before the funds are needed. Because planned giving involves assets, these gifts take time—often years—to complete. Creating relationships with donors is a long-term process, and sometimes closure is difficult to achieve. But as the relationships are built, it is important not to forget to ask for the gift!

BUILDING YOUR DONOR BASE FOR THE FUTURE

Growing a planned giving program may seem like a daunting task, but your strongest building blocks are likely already part of your fundraising structure. Annual donors and long-standing contributors are ideal candidates for your planned giving program: "Annual donors or members who become habitual contributors to your organization form the groups with the highest likelihood of becoming planned gift donors" (Henze, 2011: 2). Through active engagement and cultivation strategies, you can turn devoted annual supporters into planned giving donors.

Annual Campaign

While a planned giving program may be at the top of your fundraising pyramid, there are other key components to a strong fundraising program. The first is a large, dedicated, and engaged group of annual donors. Annual giving campaigns that are well developed and executed can build a pipeline of donors committed to your organization's goals. "Loyal giving behavior frequently trumps gift size as a predictor of planned giving" (Henze, 2011: 2). Memberships and event attendance can also act as strong indicators demonstrating loyalty linked to a potential planned gift.

Over time, we have learned the key components to a successful campaign, and we continue to learn. Our annual campaign started modestly in 2008. Appeal letters were mailed to a small pool of regular and potential donors; a small return was received. Based on this experience, strategies were re-evaluated, and money was spent outsourcing the efforts to grow our donor base through a high profile, expensive service provider. Yes, our donations increased, and a selection of new donors was established. However, the return barely offset the cost.

In 2011, the Library Foundation initiated the Buy-a-Book Club, a direct-mail annual campaign generating gifts of all sizes that directly support collections and other current needs of the library. The Buy-a-Book Club is an ideal format for the library's annual campaign as it targets annual donors and encourages loyal membership in a club that provides essential funding to support the library's collections.

The Buy-a-Book Club establishes a successful annual appeal process by providing an opportunity for devoted library supporters to feel that they are a part of a larger group of elite donors. By working to engage and cultivate annual donors, the Library Foundation generates support for collections and current library needs and cultivates our next generation of major donors. This is the donor pipeline built by annual giving.

The Future Starts Today

The pipeline built by annual giving must continue to grow. New donors can fulfill this need to an extent, but the key to sustained growth of your pipeline is building a multigenerational donor base. From the Matures Generation to Generation Y (born 1981–1995), organizations have a vast range of potential donors to target. So the question becomes, how do we reach them all?

With approximately 88 percent of all Matures annually giving to some cause or organization, it seems logical to make this group the focus of fundraising initiatives. However, with 43 percent of all dollars donated coming from the Boomers (born 1946–1964), it's also wise to analyze the reach of your current fundraising programs, how you interact with donors (phone or e-mail), and how they prefer to give (direct mail or online) (Rovner, 2013).

Traditional vs. Digital

Effective fundraising strategies change with time. In just three years, from 2010 to 2013, Baby Boomers changed their giving habits from giving primarily via direct mail to giving 42 percent online and 40 percent of the time through the mail (Rovner, 2013). As the technology era expands and forms of traditional communication decline, organizations must optimize their efforts by using a mix of strategies to reach multiple generations of donors.

The Library Foundation has worked to capitalize on the mixed-media approach with the Buy-a-Book Club campaign. The annual campaign began solely as a direct-mail appeal, including paper forms for payment, and has progressed to include online payment options. Promotions of the appeal are sent via e-mail and social media outlets. The mixed-media approach has brought yearly increases to the annual campaign, with the 2013 appeal up 40 percent from 2012 (see Figure 11.3).

An organization's goals, experiences, and donor base should guide its fundraising strategies. The optimal mix of media will vary, and it may take time to recognize the reward for your efforts. However, younger supporters are the future of all donor bases, so attracting multiple generations will help create a sustainable fundraising program and reliable sources of funding.

INFRASTRUCTURE

All of these fundraising strategies work together with the right organizational support. The Library Foundation is a 501(c)3 organization. It has two staff members: an executive director and an administrative specialist. Both positions are library employees and are assigned to staff the Library Foundation through a loaned-employee agreement. The foundation executive director reports to the library CEO.

As a separate organization, the Library Foundation also has a governing board, which sets policy, budget, provides fiscal oversight, and, in consultation with the executive director, determines how requests from the library will be funded. Much of the foundation's operational costs are borne by the foundation. The library provides office space, facilities support, technology, marketing, and other administrative support. The library also pays half of the executive director's salary and benefits.

The relationship between the library's board of trustees and the Library Foundation Board is key to the success of both institutions. Representatives from each board attend each other's meetings and report on key activities and updates on the progress of the strategic or fund development plans. The library's CEO attends all meetings, shares information on library initiatives, provides updates on the strategic plan, serves as a liaison, and helps negotiate and represent the interests of both parties. This same type of relationship exists with the Friends of the Topeka and Shawnee County Public Library.

Remember the three-legged stool? These are three interdependent organizations, each working to fulfill its responsibilities to make a great library. This structure enables each entity to pursue its individual mission, while all work together to fulfill the objectives of the library's strategic plan.

ANNUAL APPEAL COMPARISON REPORT

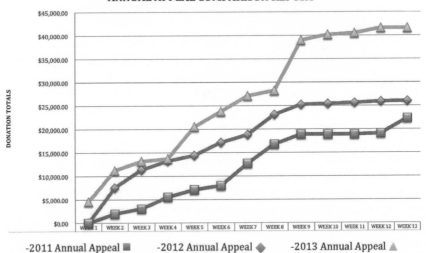

Figure 11.3. Annual appeal comparison graph. (Credit: LeAnn Meyer, administrative specialist, the Library Foundation, and Rich Kobs, art director, Topeka and Shawnee County Public Library)

CONCLUSION

Great libraries serve their communities by understanding and meeting literacy and learning needs. Great libraries need great funding. Philanthropy has and will continue to be essential in the Topeka and Shawnee County Public Library's quest to be the best library for its community. An informed and professional approach utilizing best practices will ensure continued fundraising success and a world-class library.

REFERENCES

Henze, Lawrence. 2004. "Making Planned Giving Work for You." *Blackbaud White Paper* (October): 1.

Henze, Lawrence. 2011. "Taking Control of Your Annual Fund." *Blackbaud* (April): 1–2.

Rovner, M. 2013. "The Next Generation of American Giving." *Blackbaud* (August): 5–31.

12

Digital Philanthropy and Libraries

Lee Price

Conservation Center for Art and Historic Artifacts

WHAT IS DIGITAL PHILANTHROPY?

Broad public interest in the Internet began in the 1990s. Facebook—the face of social media—was launched in 2004. Kickstarter—the face of crowdfunding—was launched in 2009. A natural product of this new age, digital philanthropy—the use of the Internet to raise funding for nonprofits and other community organizations—is in its infancy. Its potential is incalculable.

While discussion of digital philanthropy is important, it remains too early to pinpoint best practices within such a young and rapidly changing field. The term "best practices" suggests strategies that have been proven to generate consistent success. For libraries, the data simply aren't in yet. While some hypotheses have been proposed, they have not undergone rigorous testing. Therefore, the thoughts and suggestions presented here should be regarded as soft and pliable, not hard and fast. The best practices digital philanthropy rulebook for libraries is probably at least a decade down the road—and who can predict now what the digital landscape will look like at that point!

The subject of digital philanthropy is inextricably linked to the rise of social media. As it turns out, libraries of all types (public, special, and academic) are ideal centers for creating community through social media. The new social media communication channels thrive on information, and that's what libraries are all about. In 2011, I discussed opportunities for libraries to participate in social media with Colleen Dilenschneider, chief marketing engagement officer at IMPACTS and the author of the museum-focused *Know Your Own Bone* blog (www.colleendilen.com). As she noted,

When a person goes to a library they experience being there, surrounded by books and information—that's the sense of touch, in a way. Social media allows potential donors to experience the essence of the library through other senses when they are not on-location. They can listen to stories online, watch videos of library events, and create relationships by contributing their own thoughts to forums. (Price, 2011)

Several academic studies have focused upon the so-called Generation Y, or Millennials, born between the late 1970s and the early 2000s and generally considered the prime users of social media. This generation came of age in a world where computers were ubiquitous and information could be easily electronically shared between strangers through networked communities. The Millennials have been called the first "always connected" generation (Dune, 2013). As fundraising has generally focused upon established professionals and older adults with disposable income, nonprofits did not feel a strong need to quickly move into a world that was viewed as the province of the young. Strategies like crowdfunding—designed specifically for soliciting online financial contributions—have developed relatively late in the fast and turbulent evolution of the Internet. But these strategies are needed now as Millennials age into respectability—and as they reveal themselves to be quite generous.

In compiling these suggestions, I have drawn from three interesting projects that I participated in during the past three years. First, I participated as a blogger in two successful peer-to-peer blogathons that raised funding for film preservation projects. Second, the Conservation Center for Art and Historic Artifacts where I work led a crowdfunding competition in 2013 for ten collecting institutions in Pennsylvania. Participants included archives and special libraries, as well as museums and historic sites. And third, as a fundraising columnist for *Public Libraries* journal, I conducted an examination into effective website fundraising at public libraries throughout the country in 2012.

Instead of best practices, I would like to offer ten suggestions—broad generalizations that can be creatively used to point libraries in the direction of fundraising success.

1. Keep expectations reasonable.
2. Invest time in social media community building.
3. Provide flexible management for institutional social media.
4. Woo maximizers.
5. Keep discussion lively.
6. Create urgency.
7. Always keep ease of sharing in mind.

8. Streamline navigation.
9. Maintain a balance between the virtual and the real.
10. Don't try to be a master of all social media.

These are merely ten suggestions—not ten commandments. You could follow all ten and fail. You might ignore them and succeed. But I sincerely think that your odds for fundraising success will increase if you follow the suggestions.

In order to examine these ten ideas, I will begin with an overview of the tools of digital philanthropy, follow with a brief review of my three projects, and close with some further ruminations upon each of the suggestions.

THE TOOLS OF DIGITAL PHILANTHROPY

According to the Network for Good, a leading fundraising platform, the percentage of people who had made at least one donation online increased from 4 percent in 2001 to 65 percent in 2011 (Network for Good, 2011). This occurred during a period when individual, corporate, and foundation giving was relatively stagnant, and federal, state, and local government funding sources were subjected to numerous cuts (and sometimes even eliminated altogether). With each passing year, digital philanthropy came to look even more attractive to the nonprofit community. Simultaneously, donor comfort with the process of making online contributions increased, most noticeably in the immediate wake of large-scale natural disasters when appeals for assistance went viral across the major social media platforms. These campaigns created models for other nonprofit organizations to adapt.

Digital philanthropy has piggybacked on the viral potential implicit in social media. When a nonprofit organization sends out an annual appeal letter, the hope is that the potential donor will take the letter into his or her office and write a check. Then the appeal letter is filed away. End of story. But with digital philanthropy, the hope is that the receiver will share that message with neighbors, friends, and family, each one of whom will share it again with their own universe of friends—with credit cards charging donations all down the line.

Effective digital philanthropy strategies generally include use of one or more social media platforms. These are the interactive sites where visitors gather and where material is shared, opening institutions up to larger audiences and greater potential for contributions. In addition to Facebook and Twitter, social media platforms include Google+, Instagram, LinkedIn, YouTube, Pinterest, Delicious, Digg, Reddit, Flickr, Foursquare, and many others, as well as thousands of ongoing blogs (Allen-Greil, 2013).

As of early 2014, Facebook and Twitter dominate the social media landscape. You need either one or the other to go viral (a term used for the exponential spread of a meme through sharing). Facebook and Twitter hold out a promise of immediate, and largely free, access to the largest mass audience ever assembled. It's as if the 1930s *Saturday Evening Post*—or ABC, CBS, and NBC in the 1960s—started accepting free advertisements. Except Facebook and Twitter have even larger audiences than these once-dominant media giants ever enjoyed!

Digital philanthropy includes website donation pages, mobile giving, Internet competitions, peer-to-peer fundraising, and crowdfunding. The field continues to expand, shift, and morph daily. Big players abruptly rise to the surface—briefly dominating the tech news—and then disappear back into the depths. Creative entrepreneurs continuously update the rules, and early adopters set the tone.

Website Donation Pages

In 2011, blogger Colleen Dilenschneider shared the following observation with me: While an organization's own website is the best channel for online fundraising, the actual work of community formation largely takes place elsewhere. "Facebook, Twitter, Flickr, and YouTube are important channels for fundraising because they serve as portals to engage audiences while at the same time driving potential donors to the organization's website," she said. "These sites have an independent ability to build community around an organization by creatively engaging potential donors through pictures, videos and bite-sized updates, building a seemingly one-on-one relationship with the organization" (Price, 2011).

Within the past twenty years, nearly every library has designed a website. In most cases, a library website should include opportunities for visitors to make financial donations, whether toward general operating support or special projects or toward purchase of a membership in a Friends organization. Following Dilenschneider's advice, libraries should build their communities via social media and then link their followers to the main website at opportune moments.

Branding of website donation pages, as opposed to using a generic donation page, appears to be critical to success. In a 2012 report on digital philanthropy, Network for Good reported that average contribution on branded pages tended to be 20 to 30 percent larger than on generic pages (Network for Good, 2012).

Some special and academic libraries have used website pages to successfully promote programs such as Adopt-a-Book campaigns. As one example, the Friends of the Library at Mariam Coffin Canaday Library at Bryn Mawr College manage an exemplary Book Preservation Fund, allowing for the sponsorship of specific rare books in their collection (www.brynmawr.edu/library/speccoll/preservation/books/). These types of programs offer wonderful gift opportunities, similar to the popular programs that environmental organizations run to virtually adopt endangered animals such as whales, manatees, and gorillas.

Mobile Giving

Mobile devices offer opportunities for spontaneous giving. Mobile fundraising service-providers—currently including Connect2give, Give by Cell, mGive, Mobile Commons, and MobileCause—provide professional support to streamline the acceptance of microdonations. These services have been extraordinarily successful in generating immediate funding in response to large-scale disasters, such as earthquakes and hurricanes (Network for Good and PayPal, 2013). The technology is available for creative use by libraries as well.

Internet Competitions

On occasion, large corporations such as Amazon, Pepsi, and Aviva Insurance have opted to use this variation on crowdfunding in order to promote their corporate philanthropic profiles. Nonprofits and other community organizations are encouraged to compete against each other on the corporation's platform, generating heavy Internet traffic and goodwill through "sharing" and "likes." Many organizations participate, with a handful of winners taking home the big prizes. These competitions play to the strengths of nonprofit organizations with broad memberships and a committed and deep social media presence.

A more friendly variation upon this approach has been pioneered by community foundations to raise funding in a targeted area. As an example, the Minnesota Community Foundation has achieved great success with GiveMN and its annual Give to the Max Day, usually scheduled in mid-November (GiveMN, 2013). For twenty-four hours, hundreds of participating Minnesota organizations promote their causes, soliciting online contributions through a central platform, powered by Razoo, a very flexible online platform that caters to nonprofit organizations. In 2013, Give to the Max Day raised over $17 million, with the top-performing library organization—the Friends of the Hennepin County Library—netting 539 donations totaling $44,739 (http://givemn.razoo.com/giving_events/GTMD13/home).

Similar one-day campaigns have been very successful in such places as Utah, Kentucky, and Omaha, Nebraska.

The movement for #GivingTuesday, a philanthropic day to follow the post-Thanksgiving Black Friday and Cyber Monday shopping days, is promising to take this approach to a national level.

Peer-to-Peer Fundraising

New strategies are rapidly being developed to encourage supporters of organizations to host fundraising initiatives at their personal social media centers. The supporters can reach out to entirely new audiences, establishing credibility and a personal connection with the cause. The blogathons that I participated in were a variation of this approach—initiatives organized and managed by supporters rather than staff.

Crowdfunding

Crowdfunding is the art of raising donations through the Internet for a tightly defined purpose, usually over a limited period of time. In just a few years, crowdfunding platforms have revolutionized digital philanthropy. Starting in 2000, various platforms were developed to serve as centers for time-focused campaigns to raise capital for projects, but large-scale success remained elusive. The stars finally aligned in 2009 with the founding of Kickstarter, which quickly established itself as the crowdfunding industry standard. In 2010, approximately $27 million was pledged to projects on Kickstarter. Just two years later, in 2012, the total amount skyrocketed to more than $300 million (Adelman, 2013).

But while phenomenally successful, Kickstarter focused more on for-profit endeavors rather than community and nonprofit causes. This opened the field for a whole new generation of crowdfunding platforms that directly cater to organizations like public libraries, special and academic libraries, and archives. Other businesses entered the market, including Indiegogo, Crowdrise, Rockethub, Power2Give, and Razoo, with some of these sites offering more nonprofit-friendly incentives.

In the summer of 2013, the Freer and Sackler Galleries of the Smithsonian Institution launched a one-month campaign to raise $125,000 for their exhibit "Yoga: The Art of Transformation" (see Figure 12.1). The Smithsonian mounted a crowdfunding platform directly on its own website, powering it through Razoo. Through astute marketing and savvy promotion, they succeeded in blowing past their goal, raising a total of $176,415 in just thirty days. They did this by first tapping into their existing Smithsonian communi-

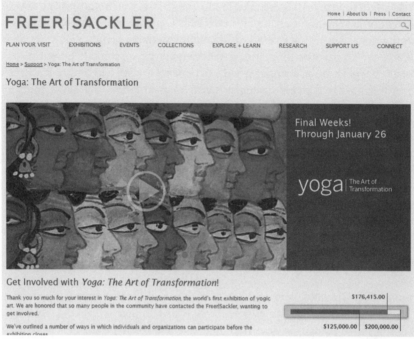

Figure 12.1. The Smithsonian Institution's "Together We're One" crowdfunding web page supporting the Freer and Sackler Galleries exhibition "Yoga: The Art of Transformation." (Credit: Krishna Vishvarupa (detail). India, Himachal Pradesh, Bilaspur, ca. 1740; Opaque watercolor and gold on paper, 19.8 x 11.7 cm; Catherine and Ralph Benkaim Collection. Source: Freer Sackler, www.asia.si.edu/)

ties, built through blogging and social media involvement, and then creatively venturing into the many online communities that center around the popular practice of yoga. Their success underlined the potential of crowdfunding for cultural fundraising.

PERSONAL EXPERIENCES IN CYBERSPACE

My family calls me a Luddite, but really I'm just a slow adopter. For years, I chose to observe quietly, keeping a discreet distance from the fray. When I finally tentatively ventured into cyberspace in the late 1990s, I discovered that there are aspects of the Internet that make intuitive sense to me. For instance, I instantly grasped the potential of blogging, Facebook, and crowdfunding for effective marketing. In 2010, I joined Facebook, started blogging six months later, and actively participated in a digital philanthropy project for the first time in 2011.

My initial positive experiences led to enthusiasm and commitment toward a rapidly growing and changing new field. I'm convinced there's huge potential here. But I'm also wary of pundits who make claims regarding their expertise. To me, the field still appears highly experimental. Even the fortunate people who are working with experienced staff and ample resources find they have to develop strategies based on assumptions that have not been fully subjected to academic research. Because the field is changing so fast, controls that would be appropriate for research purposes are difficult to apply with any rigor. Eventually, best practices for digital philanthropy will emerge from peer-reviewed research, but it may take time.

In the meantime, we have anecdotes. Here are mine.

The For the Love of Film Blogathons

In February 2011, I participated in my first peer-to-peer fundraising exercise with For the Love of Film: The Film Preservation Blogathon (see Figure 12.2). Hosted by Marilyn Ferdinand (blogger on *Ferdy on Films*) and Farran Nehme (blogger on *The Self-Styled Siren*), For the Love of Film organized approximately forty bloggers over a one-week period to raise money to conserve a 1950 film noir called *The Sound of Fury* (also known as *Try and Get Me!*), starring Lloyd Bridges of *Sea Hunt* fame (Nehme, 2011).

I participated through two of my blogs—*Preserving a Family Collection* (preservingafamilycollection.blogspot.com) and *June and Art* (juneandart .blogspot.com), a short-term blog on which I posted the love letters exchanged by my parents during their 1949–1951 courtship. For the blogathon, I spent one week writing about the movies my parents watched and the challenges of preserving film material in home collections. Each blog entry featured a prominently placed donation button, which linked directly to the Film Noir Foundation contribution page. In that one week, with around forty bloggers blogging away, we raised over $5,000, significantly contributing toward restoration of the film (Ferdinand, 2012). The restored version premiered at the San Francisco Film Noir Festival in 2013 (Ferdinand, 2013).

In 2012 we did it again, as For the Love of Film turned to the legacy of Alfred Hitchcock (see Figure 12.3). This time, the objective was to make the recently discovered silent film *The White Shadow* (1923) accessible to the public by preparing it for live streaming on the Internet and adding an original musical score. While the forty-minute *The White Shadow* was incomplete, the existing footage inspired great interest among classic film fans because of Alfred Hitchcock's early participation as set designer, screenwriter, and assistant director (he would complete his move to the director's chair the following year). Each blogathon entry linked to a special contribution page of the National Film Preservation Foundation.

Figure 12.2.   Preserving a Family Collection web page promoting For the Love of Film: The Film Preservation Blogathon (February 16, 2011). (Source: *Preserving a Family Collection* blog, preservingafamilycollection.blogspot.com)

I contributed with daily blog entries on my personal blog *21 Essays* (21es says.blogspot.com)—writing six essays on Alfred Hitchcock's film *Blackmail* (1929). With 112 bloggers participating, we raised $6,490 in a week for the National Film Preservation Foundation (Ferdinand, 2013). A generous matching grant from the on-demand independent film service Fandor completed the fundraising project, and the restored footage was made publicly accessible for the first time since the 1920s, running on both the National Film Preservation Foundation and Fandor websites.

Pennsylvania's Top 10 Endangered Artifacts

At the Conservation Center for Art and Historic Artifacts, where I work as director of development, we built our own crowdfunding platform in 2013. It was designed to add a fundraising component to Pennsylvania's Top 10 En-

Figure 12.3. Promotion button, designed by blogger Roderick Heath, for the 2012 For the Love of Film: Film Preservation Blogathon. (Source: *For the Love of Film*, www. moviepreservation.blogspot.com/)

dangered Artifacts, a competition modeled on a successful Top 10 program managed by the Virginia Association of Museums and the well-established America's 11 Most Endangered Historic Places program run by the National Trust for Historic Preservation. While both programs strongly encouraged fundraising efforts by the represented institutions, neither offered a centrally based crowdfunding platform.

As a fundraising professional, I was particularly interested in this project because it essentially created a laboratory in which to observe crowdfunding strategies enacted by ten relatively similar organizations. They were given six weeks to reach fundraising goals needed to conserve their endangered artifacts. The platform was launched at noon on September 19, 2013, during a special event at the governor's mansion in Harrisburg, Pennsylvania. With the platform unveiled, fundraising began in earnest.

For Pennsylvania's Top 10 Endangered Artifacts, we opted to create our own crowdfunding platform (see Figure 12.4) rather than use the commercially available platforms, such as Kickstarter and Indiegogo. We applied for grant assistance from a local foundation to create the platform and support

Figure 12.4. The crowdfunding web page for the 2013 Pennsylvania's Top 10 Endangered Artifacts campaign, managed by the Conservation Center for Art and Historic Artifacts. (Source: Conservation Center for Art and Historic Artifacts, www.ccaha.org)

promotional efforts. With grant funding in hand, we enlisted a website design firm to assist in creating a new crowdfunding website dedicated to collections care projects. We wanted the user-friendly ease of the standard crowdfunding model married to a design that meshed with the preservation-focused mission of the Conservation Center. We wanted our platform to reflect a love of history and art even as it tempted casual observers to contribute.

In its design, the platform emphasized photographic images over videos because we wanted to keep our platform accessible to organizations that might not have the resources to produce a polished video. And we built in a backdoor so we could count contributions that went directly to the organization (as opposed to online contributions). The result was a crowdfunding platform that at first glance might look like a Kickstarter or Indiegogo page but—on closer examination—revealed itself to be considerably more nonprofit, and collections care, friendly.

The platform design nicely complemented the objectives of Pennsylvania's Top 10 Endangered Artifacts, which was conceived as something different from the standard Internet popularity contest. We used a peer-review process to select the ten artifacts, convening a panel of judges, representative of all regions in the state and with deep experience in history and art. The panel reviewed nominations for sixty organizations and then met at the Conservation Center to whittle the contestants down to ten. At the end of a day filled with intense deliberations, the panel emerged with a list of ten remarkable artifacts.

The ten competing institutions were the Academy of Natural Sciences of Drexel University; the American Philatelic Society; the Carnegie Museum of Art; the Chester County Historical Society; LancasterHistory.org; the Mennonite Heritage Center; Old Economy Village; the Pennsylvania Academy of the Fine Arts; the Pennsylvania Anthracite Heritage Museum; and the Schwenkfelder Library and Heritage Center.

At the conclusion of the six-week campaign period, the winner of the most votes would receive the People's Choice Award. But more importantly, all would get to keep the money raised for their artifacts on the crowdfunding platform, including an initial contribution to each campaign from a regional corporate foundation. There would be no losers in this fundraising competition.

Each of the institutions received support in developing marketing strategies from a full-service communications firm. Collections care initiatives rarely receive opportunities for statewide promotion (or, for that matter, nationwide publicity when the Associated Press picks up the story!). Thanks to Pennsylvania's Top 10 Endangered Artifacts, ten amazing pieces in important Pennsylvania collections were widely recognized for their historical and artistic significance.

Responding to the challenge of crowdfunding, some of the institutions became creative in their strategies. LancasterHistory.org held a Thaddeus

Stevens look-alike contest to raise votes and funding to preserve their Civil War–era Thaddeus Stevens wig. The Chester County Historical Society hosted a click-a-thon at a local restaurant to raise awareness of their campaign for the Passmore Williamson guest book, a treasured artifact of the abolitionist movement. Others used Facebook and Twitter to spread the word.

At the Conservation Center, we are still engaged in a review of the impact of Pennsylvania's Top 10 Endangered Artifacts. Over six weeks, the ten campaigns brought in 5.2 million votes and over $16,000 for collections care initiatives. There was no downside. The ten artifacts received more attention than ever before, along with an infusion of money for their long-term preservation.

The Website Clinic

My growing interest in digital philanthropy prompted me to engage in a close examination of the fundraising components of public library websites. As research for a column for *Public Libraries* journal, I reviewed the fifty-five American public library websites that were listed (as of April 29, 2012) in the Library Website Hall of Fame located on the Website Design page of Library Success: A Best Practices Wiki. The column, titled "The Website Clinic," was published in the July/August 2012 issue of *Public Libraries* (Price, 2012).

Of the fifty-five websites, my initial examination revealed that twenty-four prominently featured a fundraising component above the fold (defined as the portion of the website that is visible on an average computer monitor without scrolling downward). My assumption was that if fundraising was valued by the library, I would see some solicitation within this space. I looked for the words "Give" or "Donate" or "Support" somewhere above the fold.

Then, on each of the twenty-four websites, I counted the number of clicks that had to be made to reach the point of donation. Naturally, the fewer clicks, the better. With each additional click, the library runs the risk of losing the potential donor.

I docked points for Give buttons that emphasized volunteering or donations of books over financial contributions. While these areas may be of great importance to the library, the positioning implied that fundraising was a secondary function. Also, I docked points for Give buttons with dropdown options for going to a Friends or a Foundation page. These options seemed insufficiently streamlined to me. In addition, they jarringly navigated the visitor off the library website.

In the cases in which there was a separate library foundation that handled the fundraising, I expected to find the two websites working smoothly together. But this was not always the case. I looked at one website where the foundation was promoting a major event to benefit the library, but there was no mention of the event on the main library website!

Finally, I assigned points for websites that offered the option of making a secure donation through a credit card. The sites that required printing and mailing a PDF form accompanied by a check required a time commitment well beyond the norm in our new digital age.

Ultimately, I narrowed the field to five exemplary fundraising websites, with the caveat that my decisions were entirely based upon the appearance of these websites on one afternoon in April 2012. The highlighted exemplary fundraising websites are below (in alphabetical order):

1. Carnegie Library of Pittsburgh (Pennsylvania) ran a bold and attractive fundraising campaign called the Perfect Match, which took up one-third of the visible page. The Click Here to Donate button delivered you directly to the donation page.
2. The Enoch Pratt Free Library (Baltimore, Maryland) featured a Support Us tab that linked to an attractively designed page focused on a specific need: "It costs $60 to sponsor a child for a whole summer's worth of library programs. Please *sponsor* one or more children and help reduce summer slide!" This is a very effective fundraising pitch.
3. The Kalamazoo Public Library (Michigan) placed an emphasis on larger gifts on their Support the Library page. Their Planned Gifts section was particularly well designed, including a Value Calculator that translated a patron's estimated use of the library into financial terms and a Donor Wall of Honor celebrating past major donors to the library.
4. The New York Public Library website was singularly uncluttered—with perhaps the fewest words of any of the fifty-five websites reviewed for this exercise. While their Support the Library link was fittingly prominent, I was most impressed with their push for earned income through a seasonally appropriate (Mother's Day) button for Unique Gifts for Mom, which linked to the library shop.
5. The High Plains Library District (Greeley, Colorado), located north of Denver, incorporated the most effective use of video, utilizing a thirty-second video produced by the American Library Association that worked in tandem with an attractive support page.

THE TEN SUGGESTIONS

There's still a sense of adventure about digital philanthropy. It's a largely uncharted country. Returning to my ten suggestions, I suggest viewing them more as a compass than a map. Each suggestion points you in a certain direction, but ultimately your institution will have to blaze its own unique path.

1. Keep Expectations Reasonable

It seems that everyone's heard of a Kickstarter campaign that raised millions, seemingly overnight. Whatever that campaign was, it was the exception—not the rule. Many crowdfunding campaigns fail, most raise less than $5,000, and funding is usually tightly earmarked for a specific, one-time project. Library stakeholders should never regard digital philanthropy as a substitute for traditional funding sources. At best, it can be an effective supplement. Nevertheless, a smartly conceived digital philanthropy campaign can be remarkably successful in funding tightly focused special programs, especially when they resonate with strong emotional appeal for targeted segments of the community.

When digital philanthropy campaigns are launched, key stakeholders should know that their involvement is essential at the early stages. Success breeds success in Internet fundraising, just as in traditional fundraising. Someone has to give first, and the initial donations are most easily made by the people closest to the institution. Trustees, Friends, and even staff should be encouraged to donate in the opening hours and then to share the information far and wide through every social media platform that they have at their disposal.

2. Invest Time in Social Media Community Building

Successful fundraising builds upon effective marketing and communications. This is as true for digital philanthropy as it has always been true for traditional philanthropy. If libraries want to succeed with digital philanthropy campaigns, they have to be willing to invest staff and volunteer time in building virtual communities through sites like Facebook and Twitter. Cross-posting across platforms increases your potential reach, although you should be careful to adjust your tone or focus to meet the expectations of each platform (Allen-Greil, 2013). The task of building a community takes time, ideally starting months or even years before the launching of ambitious fundraising campaigns. Fully engage your followers on an emotional level first—let them feel some ownership within your community—before moving on to the fundraising request.

As of early 2014, libraries remain relatively minor players in digital philanthropy, largely because so many of them have not made this basic investment in virtual community building. While viral success on the Internet will always be unpredictable, the odds will remain on the side of those who patiently lay the groundwork.

3. Provide Flexible Management for Institutional Social Media

Library management should set the tone for institutional social media (the library's official Facebook page, its Twitter account, a blog for the children's department, etc.) and should provide oversight to ensure the consistency of an appropriate institutional voice. However, in most cases, management of social media should remain unusually loose, only resorting to direct hands-on control, or even censorship, in extreme cases. The need for balance between management and edginess was addressed by Joe Murphy, a library consultant specializing in library futures who blogs at joemurphylibraryfuture.com, when I interviewed him in 2011. "A point person ensures quality control," Murphy said. "But ultimately it should be a community endeavor. Try being flexible in how these projects are staffed" (Price, 2011).

For best results, social media thrives on risk. In one of the most successful nonprofit crowdfunding campaigns to date, the Tesla Science Center at Wardenclyffe allowed Matthew Inman, creator of the popular Internet site *The Oatmeal*, free rein to create a social media campaign for them. Inman's edgy headline "Let's Build a Goddamn Tesla Museum" swiftly went viral. While this isn't appropriate language for an annual appeal or a grant request, it must fall within any new best practices guidelines for digital philanthropy. Inman's campaign on the crowdfunding platform Indiegogo raised $1.37 million for the Tesla Science Center (www.indiegogo.com/ projects/let-s-build-a-goddamn-tesla-museum).

4. Woo Maximizers

Georgetown University's Center for Social Impact Communication and Waggener Edstrom (2013) coined the term "Maximizer" in their report "Digital Persuasion: How Social Media Motivates Action and Drives Support for Causes." As they describe it, "Maximizers are a relatively rare breed. . . . But if you have a Maximizer in your midst, you'll know it—and appreciate it. Maximizers go all out to support the causes they care about—online, offline, and everything in between."

During that first For the Love of Film blogathon that I participated in, we were fortunate enough to engage one of the most powerful Maximizers in the country. The late film critic Roger Ebert tweeted our blogathon, blogged about it, and provided some of the perks—the prizes offered as incentives for giving that function as the crowdfunding equivalent of the PBS tote bag.

Identify and cultivate potential Maximizers within your library's social media community. They are the people with a gift for igniting discussion on the Internet. They are the people with Twitter followings measured in the thousands, tens of thousands, or even hundreds of thousands. It would be wise to consider Maximizer qualifications when looking for people to serve as trustees or board or committee members.

5. Keep Discussion Lively

On social media sites, colloquial language beats academic. Unlike the writing of, say, federal grant requests (the most analytical of all fundraising tasks), digital philanthropy is ruled by right-brain thinking. It's random, intuitive, holistic, and synthesizing. It's emotion-driven. The goal is to design material that gets the potential donor's brain to start pumping endorphins, dopamine, serotonin—the happiness neurochemicals. Cats will always be more popular than cataloging. So lead with the cat.

Ultimately, interesting topics, written with intelligence and wit, generate true community. Discussion should be encouraged, whether on blogs, Facebook, or Twitter. There is a great deal of information (including lengthy books) on the subject of search engine optimization (SEO), but the algorithms used by major search engines like Google change so quickly that even the most sophisticated corporations have difficulty keeping up. If you succeed in uncovering a secret formula for using certain words or links to raise your Internet profile, it will probably change within the month, leaving you back where you started. In the end, original and engaging content will remain your best friend in building a community.

6. Create Urgency

Digital philanthropy campaigns work best in short bursts of extremely focused giving. Minnesota's Give to the Max Day raises millions of dollars in twenty-four hours. The For the Love of Film blogathons raised thousands in a single week. Conversely, the Conservation Center's Pennsylvania's Top 10 Endangered Artifacts program ran for six weeks in 2013. Following the campaign period, more than half of the ten participating institutions expressed that the six-week period was too long. They lost that sense of urgency that makes these campaigns both effective and fun. Lesson learned: Keep it short.

Within a fundraising campaign, matching grant opportunities can be used on crowdfunding initiatives in much the same way as matching grants are used during public television and radio pledge drives. In these situations, the library would solicit a matching contribution from a corporation, foundation, or major donor, making the contribution contingent on raising a certain amount of money within a limited period of time. The public radio and television stations use this technique for a good reason: it works. According to the "2013 Millennial Impact Report," the third highest reason that Millennials reported for online giving in 2012 was the assurance that their contribution would be matched by another source (Achieve Guidance, 2013). Within a crowdfunding campaign, this approach must be planned to coincide with a heavy e-mail and social media push because the time to get the word out is very limited. (Note: Save your e-mail blasts for moments of critical urgency such as this. According to Achieve Guidance, authors of the "2013 Millennial Impact Report," 71.5 percent of Millennials complain that nonprofits e-mail them too frequently.)

7. Always Keep Ease of Sharing in Mind

Since you want people to share your digital philanthropy initiatives, you must think about the type of material that tends to be shared on the Internet. Respondents to the "2013 Millennial Impact Report" stated a preference for images and videos rather than straight text. For this reason, libraries should be on the alert for opportunities to promote their initiatives through strong visuals. Collect photographs, graphics, and videos in advance and file them away for use. Above all, identify a talented amateur videographer from your staff or volunteer pool to be on call to film and edit short videos that celebrate your library's work.

Keep in mind that the act of sharing is very personal. When people choose to share an item, they are aware (at least subliminally) that this item is contributing to their virtual persona—the material that we share on status updates on Facebook or by retweeting on Twitter defines the way that distant friends imagine us. Therefore, libraries should provide sharable material that is upbeat and easily personalized. Always look for lively connections between your collections and the outside world—acknowledge holidays, remember anniversaries, and find links with national and international news that will remind followers of the relevancy of your collections.

That basic building block of Internet communication—the e-mail—is vitally important in sharing as well. Especially as campaigns reach their climax, personalized e-mails targeted toward the most likely donors can be extraordinarily effective in generating larger contributions. This approach is particularly important in crowdfunding endeavors. Even people who have already given to the crowdfunding initiative can be thanked again via e-mail, informed of the current status of the campaign, and then asked to give one last time—with a direct link to the donation page.

8. Streamline Navigation

Click, click, click . . . You lose viewers with each click that's required to reach the donation page. There should be a clear and easy path to the donation. One click is best, two clicks is acceptable, three clicks is not recommended, and more than three clicks is disastrous. In addition, the navigation should be user-friendly on smartphones and other mobile technology. According to the

"2013 Millennial Impact Report," 76 percent of Millennials complain about the difficulties of navigating mobile-friendly sites (Achieve Guidance, 2013). Never annoy your potential donor. Ease of navigation is essential.

When a campaign is under way, donation links should be clearly visible on all major pages of the website, ideally even appearing in the same location on the screen to allow for an aesthetically pleasing visual continuity. Savvy organizations like the New York Public Library will place the same banner on all their hundreds of pages during short-term critical fundraising or advocacy campaigns (Price, 2011). They know what they're doing—and their approach can be easily emulated by much smaller organizations. (Another tip: Watch what the big guys are doing.)

9. Maintain a Balance between the Virtual and the Real

Especially when working with a bricks-and-mortar institution like a library, look for opportunities to link back to reality. Your virtual supporters should be encouraged to show up at the building. Digital philanthropy initiatives can, and should, be supported by real-life events in which people can mingle, meet staff, hear the passion, and write the checks. When developing a campaign, remember that there should be a multipronged approach in which digital philanthropy is just one important piece in the puzzle.

10. Don't Try to Be a Master of All Social Media

In her 2013 Heritage Preservation webinar "Promoting Preservation: Utilizing New Media," photograph conservator Heather Brown recommended focusing energy on just one or two social media platforms, developing your presence on the ones that feel best suited to your institution. Then follow other institutions to see how they are implementing their social media strategies. In the case of libraries, look for the library systems that are realizing success in the social media arena through building large numbers of followers or the leading of successful online fundraising campaigns. Do what they do.

While it may be exciting to be an early adopter of new technologies, it's also perfectly acceptable to be a late adopter. The important thing is to find the platforms where you can interact most easily with a potentially large and enthusiastic community. Some new technologies and platforms burn bright fast and then flare out. Others never catch on, regardless of their perceived quality or innovations. For maximum marketing effect, you want to position your organization with the most popular platforms.

Maybe the biggest places—the New York Public Library or the Boston Public Library—can maintain mastery over a dozen or more social media platforms. But most medium-to-small-size systems can manage to be extremely effective by concentrating on just a few channels. At this point, Facebook is most important, with Twitter standing second in line. Build your communities where your organization feels most comfortable and where your patrons and followers are most likely to congregate virtually. Keep track of the trends, but don't feel an urge to jump on them early. The most important thing is to maintain interest and enthusiasm among your followers.

CONCLUSION

Fundraising is all about relationship-building, and the new world of social media offers ideal tools for cultivation. As patrons become more fully engaged, they grow in their potential to be forceful advocates and enthusiastic donors. The technology is new but the strategy is classic: Cultivate, cultivate, cultivate . . . and then ask for a contribution.

ACKNOWLEDGMENT

Special thanks to Katie Dune for her research assistance with this chapter.

REFERENCES

Achieve Guidance. 2013. "2013 Millennial Impact Report." www.themillennialim
    pact.com/2013research.
Adelman, Bob. 2013. "Kickstarter Marks Another Milestone." *The New American*. www.thenewamerican.com/economy/markets/item/16848-kickstarter-marks
    -another-milestone.
Allen-Greil, Dana. 2013. "Engaging Audiences with Social Media." Webinar presented by Heritage Preservation. www.connectingtocollections.org/courses/
    outreach-activities-for-collections-care/.
Brown, Heather, and Samantha Skelton. 2013. "Promoting Preservation: Utilizing New Media." Webinar presented by Heritage Preservation. www.connectingto
    collections.org/newmedia/.
Dune, Katie. 2013. *Cultivating the Millennial Online Donor*. Thesis submitted to the Department of Museum Studies, the University of the Arts, Philadelphia, PA.
Ferdinand, Marilyn. 2012. "The Blogathon Is Officially Toes Up." *Ferdy on Films*. www.ferdyonfilms.com/2012/the-blogathon-is-officially-toes-up/14453/.
Ferdinand, Marilyn. 2013. "*Try and Get Me!* (aka *The Sound of Fury*, 1950)." *Ferdy on Films*. www.ferdyonfilms.com/2013/try-and-get-me-aka-the-sound-of
    -fury-1950/17482/.

Georgetown University and Waggener Edstrom. 2013. "Digital Persuasion: How Social Media Motivates Action and Drives Support for Causes." http://waggener edstrom.com/what-we-do/social-innovation/report-digital-persuasion/.

GiveMN. 2013. "Give to the Max Day." http://givemn.razoo.com/giving_events/ GTMD13/home.

Nehme, Farran. 2011. "For the Love of Film (Noir): Let the Links Begin." *The Self-Styled Siren.* http://selfstyledsiren.blogspot.com/2011/02/for-love-of-film-noir-let -links-begin.html.

Network for Good. 2011. *Annual Report.* www1.networkforgood.org/sites/default/ files/nfg_annual_report_2011_final.pdf.

Network for Good. 2012. *The Network for Good Digital Giving Index, Q3 2012.* www.fundraising123.org/files/Community/NFGDigitalGivingIndexQ32012.pdf.

Network for Good and PayPal. 2013. "Why Mobile Matters: A Guide to the Mobile Web." http://learn.networkforgood.org/mobile.html.

Price, Lee. 2011. "Social Media Brings in the Money." *Public Libraries* 50, no. 2 (March/April 2011): 24–27.

Price, Lee. 2012. "The Website Clinic." *Public Libraries* 51, no. 4 (July/August 2012): 25–27.

Index

About the Contributors

Sidney Berger is Ann C. Pingree director of the Phillips Library, Peabody Essex Museum, Salem, Massachusetts; professor, GSLIS, Simmons College, Boston; and professor, GSLIS, University of Illinois, Urbana/Champaign.

Terry R. Collings was the Seattle Public Library's first development professional, having served as their foundation's executive director for eighteen years before retiring in 2007. Before moving to Seattle, he worked for three years at the Denver Public Library, raising funds for the acquisition and preservation of materials in the Denver Public Library's Western History collection. Terry has a BA in government and an MA in education from Indiana University coupled with an MBA from the University of Denver.

Kurt H. Cumiskey earned his MLIS from the University of Wisconsin, Milwaukee, and an MA in literature from the University of Central Florida. He served on the editorial board of *College and Research Libraries* and as chair of several committees of the ALA International Relations Roundtable, and he has written book reviews for *Library Journal* for several years. He is now assistant director of development at Duke University Libraries, with responsibilities for the Annual Fund, planned giving, and foundation and corporation grants.

Mary E. Edwards is the distance learning and liaison librarian at the University of Florida Health Science Center Library, where she has worked since 2004. Mary holds an MA from the University of South Florida in library and information science, and she earned an EdD in educational technology from the University of Florida.

Thomas B. Hadzor is associate university librarian for development at Duke University. He holds an MA in higher education administration from Michigan State University and an undergraduate degree from Muhlenberg College. He did his high school work at Mercersburg Academy. Over a thirty-five-year development career, he has served two independent secondary schools, a small college, and three different programs at Duke. Tom has also worked with a number of nonprofit organizations and boards over the years while raising six children.

Karlene Noel Jennings is a consultant with Dominion Library Associates and served as a library development director for academic libraries for twelve years. She is past chair of ALADN and past facilitator of DORAL. She holds an MSIS from the University of Tennessee, Knoxville, and a PhD from Iowa State University. She is a certified fundraising executive and a member of ALA. As of January 2014, Karlene serves the College of William & Mary in Virginia as senior director of scholarships and special projects.

Andy Kahan is Ruth W. and A. Morris Williams, Jr., director of Author Events at the Free Library of Philadelphia. He has directed the Author Events Series since the turn of the millennium. In the previous century, he worked as a web editor, adjunct instructor, film electrician, bookstore manager, bartender, and researcher.

LeAnn Meyer is development administrative specialist for the Library Foundation in Topeka, Kansas. Prior to this, she worked as associate marketing director for the Kansas State University School of Music, Theatre, and Dance, where she simultaneously earned an MA. After spending her start-up years in academia, she is excited to progress her passion for nonprofit development with the Topeka and Shawnee County Public Library, an organization that undoubtedly supports lifetime learning.

Gina Millsap is chief executive officer of the Topeka and Shawnee County Public Library in Topeka, Kansas. Gina has worked in libraries for thirty-nine years and received her MLS from the University of Missouri. Her degree may be an antique, but her outlook isn't; she's been recognized as a *Library Journal* Mover and Shaker (www.libraryjournal.com:article:CA6423399.html) and is past president of the Library Leadership and Management Association (www.ala.org/ala/mgrps/divs/llama/index.cfm), a division of the American Library Association. She presents and writes on a variety of current topics, including community leadership, fundraising, market segmentation, public library trustee education, twenty-first-century librarianship, and process improvement. She is an experienced facilitator for library and community groups.

Christina Muracco is director of advancement for the Smithsonian Libraries. Tina began her fundraising career at the Pennsylvania State University Libraries, and she has served as director of development at the Catholic University of America in Washington, DC. Tina earned her BA in media studies at Pennsylvania State University and her JD from Widener University School of Law.

Hannah F. Norton is a reference and liaison librarian at the University of Florida Health Science Center Library, serving primarily as liaison to the College of Veterinary Medicine, the Department of Medicine, and the College of Medicine Class of 2015. Hannah holds an MS in information studies from the University of Texas, Austin.

Lee Price served as a contributing editor for *Public Libraries* magazine, writing the "Bringing in the Money" fundraising column from 2008 to 2012. He is the director of development at the Conservation Center for Art and Historic Artifacts (Philadelphia) and has worked as a fundraising consultant for many libraries, archives, and museums.

Jane Rutledge lives in West Lafayette, Indiana, where she is a long-time volunteer for the Friends of the Tippecanoe County Public Library. She was a founding member of Friends of Kansas Libraries and has served Friends of Indiana Libraries in several capacities, including membership chair and newsletter editor. For several years she was the editor of the Friends of Libraries USA (now United for Libraries) newsletter, and she also managed its website.

Nina Stoyan-Rosenzweig is the founding archivist and historian for the Health Science Center Libraries and J. Hillis Miller Health Science Center. Her background includes graduate work at the University of Pennsylvania and University of Michigan. Her work includes running the Health Science Center archives, developing exhibits, and teaching in the history of medicine.

Dwain Posey Teague is major gift officer for East Carolina University Libraries. Dwain's seventeen years of experience in fundraising has focused mostly on academic library fundraising. In addition to his work with the East Carolina University Library system, he previously oversaw development efforts for the School of Information and Library Science at the University of

North Carolina, Chapel Hill, as well as the university libraries at the University of Central Florida and North Carolina State University. He coauthored an article for *Technical Services Quarterly* titled "Reconnect with Your Alumni and Connect to Donors."

Michele R. Tennant is the assistant director of the Health Science Center Library, heading the Biomedical and Health Information Services Department, and bioinformatics librarian for the Genetics Institute at the University of Florida. Michele received her PhD in biology from Wayne State University and her MLIS from the University of California, Los Angeles.

Jonna Ward is executive director of the Seattle Public Library Foundation. She joined the Seattle Public Library Foundation in 2001, where she was responsible for the Community Phase of the $83 million Capital Campaign. Her charge was to build a community-wide donor base, which she did by securing over 22,000 donors to support the Campaign for Seattle's Public Libraries. She was promoted to deputy director in 2004 and became executive director in 2008. As executive director, she is responsible for all aspects of the foundation, including development, asset management, and operations.

M. Sandra Wood is librarian emerita, Pennsylvania State University Libraries. She was a librarian for over thirty-five years at the George T. Harrell Library, Milton S. Hershey Medical Center, Pennsylvania State University, specializing in reference, education, and database services.